Best Easy Day Hikes Series

Best Easy Day Hikes
Mount Rainier
National Park

Second Edition

Heidi Schneider
Mary Skjelset

FALCONGUIDE®

GUILFORD, CONNECTICUT
HELENA, MONTANA
AN IMPRINT OF THE GLOBE PEQUOT PRESS

Contents

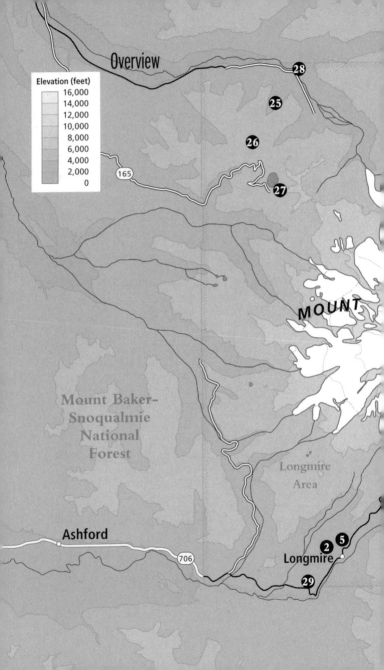

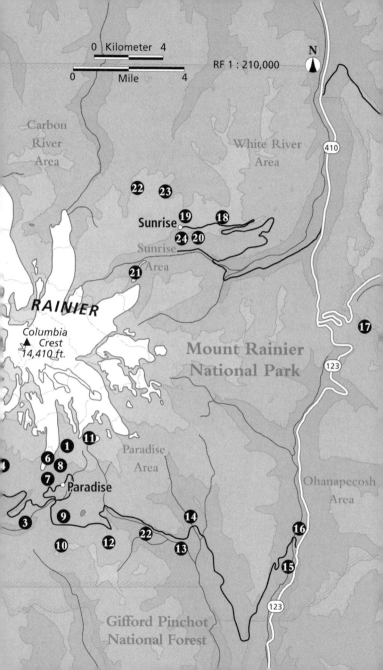

Map Legend

Boundaries

National/Wilderness Boundary `//////`

Transportation

State Highway `——(41)——`

Primary Roads `————`

Other Roads `————`

Unpaved Road `════`

Unimproved Road `= = = = =`

Featured Unpaved Road `═══`

Featured Trail `▬ ▬ ▬ ▬`

Other Trail `- - - - - -`

Nature Trail `• • • • • • •`

Off-trail Hike `· · · · · · ·`

Tunnel `—|——|—`

Hydrology

River/Creek

Intermittent Stream

Spring ℗

Falls ∥

Lake

Glacier

Marsh/Swamp

Physiography

Cavern/Natural Bridge ∩

Cliff

Pass)(

Peak ▲

Symbols

Trailhead 🚶

Trail Locator ❶

Trail Turnaround ↻

Parking 🅿

Ranger Station

Visitor Center ❓

Back Country Campground ▲

Campground △

Cabin/Lodge ↑

Picnic Area

Town ○

Viewpoint 👁

Point of Interest ■

Museum 🏛

Gate •—•

Bridge ≍

What Is a "Best Easy Day Hike"?

Best Easy Day Hikes Mount Rainier includes short, less-strenuous hikes that we recommend for nice, casual day hikes in the park.

These hikes vary in length, but most are short. With a few exceptions, none have severe hills. All hikes are on easy-to-follow trails with no off-trail sections. It is also easy to get to the trailhead of all hikes in this book; you can reach them with any two-wheel-drive vehicle.

Some of the hikes in this book might not seem easy to some hikers. To help you decide, we have ranked the hikes from easiest to hardest. Please keep in mind that short does not always equal easy. Other factors such as elevation gain and trail conditions have to be considered.

We hope you thoroughly enjoy your "best easy" hiking experiences in Mount Rainier National Park.

—Heidi Schneider and Mary Skjelset

Ranking the Hikes

The following list ranks the hikes in this book from easiest to hardest.

Box Canyon
Trail of the Shadows
Twin Firs Loop
Silver Forest
Chenuis Falls
Grove of the Patriarchs
Nisqually Vista
Sourdough Ridge Nature Trail
Alta Vista Summit
Dead Horse Creek
Silver Falls
Emmons Moraine
High Lakes Trail
Stevens Creek
Snow Lake
Narada Falls
Spray Falls
Green Lake and Ranger Falls
Dege Peak
Pinnacle Peak Saddle
Naches Peak
Mount Fremont Lookout
Sunrise Rim
Forest Lake
Paradise Glacier
Tolmie Peak
Comet Falls
Rampart Ridge
Skyline Trail

Zero Impact

Going into a national park such as Mount Rainier is like visiting a museum. You obviously do not want to leave your mark on an art treasure in the museum. If everybody going through the museum left one little mark, the piece of art would be quickly destroyed—and of what value is a big building full of trashed art? The same goes for a pristine wilderness such as Mount Rainier National Park, which is as magnificent as any masterpiece by any artist. If we all left just one little mark on the landscape, the wilderness would soon be despoiled.

A wilderness can accommodate human use as long as everybody behaves, but a few thoughtless or uninformed visitors can ruin it for everybody who follows. All wilderness users have a responsibility to know and follow the rules of zero-impact camping.

Nowadays most wilderness users want to walk softly, but some are not aware that they have poor manners. Often their actions are dictated by the outdated habits of a past generation of campers, who cut green boughs for evening shelters, built campfires with fire rings, and dug trenches around tents. These "camping rules" may have been acceptable in the 1950s, but they leave long-lasting scars. Today such behavior is absolutely unacceptable. The wilderness is shrinking, and the number of users is mushrooming. More and more camping areas show unsightly signs of heavy use.

A new code of ethics is growing out of the necessity of coping with the unending waves of people who want an enjoyable wilderness experience. Today we all must leave no clues that we have gone before. Canoeists can look behind the canoe and see no trace of their passing. Hikers, mountain bikers, and four-wheelers should have the same goal. Enjoy the wildness, but have zero impact on the landscape.

Three Falcon Zero-Impact Principles

- Leave with everything you brought.
- Leave no sign of your visit.
- Leave the landscape as you found it.

Most of us know better than to litter-in or out of the wilderness. Be sure you leave nothing, regardless of how small it is, along the trail or at the campsite. Pack out everything, including orange peels, flip tops, cigarette butts, and gum wrappers. Also pick up any trash that others have left behind.

- Follow the main trail. Avoid cutting switchbacks and walking on vegetation beside the trail.
- Do not pick up "souvenirs," such as rocks, antlers, or wildflowers. The next person wants to see them, too, and collecting such souvenirs violates park regulations.
- Avoid making loud noises that may disturb others. Remember, sound travels easily to the other side of lakes. Be courteous.
- Carry a lightweight trowel to bury human waste 6 to 8 inches deep, and pack out used toilet paper. Keep human waste at least 300 feet from any water source.
- Finally, and perhaps most important, strictly follow the pack-in/pack-out rule. If you carry something into the backcountry, consume it or carry it out.

Practice zero-impact principles—and put your ear to the ground in the wilderness and listen carefully. Thousands of people coming behind you are thanking you for your courtesy and good sense.

Getting There

Mount Rainier is located in central-western Washington and has four entrance stations—one at each corner of the park. The southwest entrance, Nisqually Entrance Station, is open year-round. The other three—Carbon River Entrance Station (northwest), Stevens Canyon Entrance Station (southeast), and White River Entrance Station (northeast)—are generally open mid- to late June or early July. It is an easy drive from Seattle, Tacoma, or Portland to any of the four entrance stations. It is also possible to fly into either Portland or the Seattle/Tacoma airport, where you can rent a car, take a shuttle, or ride a bus into the park. Although paved and well maintained, the park roads are winding two-lanes and often crowded with traffic, including slow-moving vehicles. During the daytime, expect a leisurely drive through the park.

Following is a detailed description of how to reach each entrance station.

Stevens Canyon Entrance Station: From the north (Seattle or Tacoma), go south on Interstate 5 until you reach Highway 512, which originates in Tacoma. Go east on Highway 512 to Highway 410. The park entrance is 33.0 miles from Enumclaw. Go east on Highway 410, which starts going east and then bends south as it nears the park. After entering the park, continue on Highway 410 east for 9.0 miles until the Highway 123 junction. Turn right (south) onto Highway 123 and travel for 11.2 miles to Stevens Canyon Road. Turn right (west) onto Stevens Canyon Road; the Stevens Canyon Entrance Station is directly in front of you. *DeLorme: Washington Atlas and Gazetteer:* Page 48 C4.

From the south (Portland), go about 80 miles north on I–5 to U.S. Highway 12. Go east on US 12 through Packwood (the last town—and gas, camping supplies, etc.—before entering the park), and continue 7.0 miles to Highway 123. Go left (north) on Highway 123 and in 3.0 miles enter Mount Rainier National Park. In another mile go left (west) on Stevens Canyon Road; the entrance station is directly in front of you. *DeLorme: Washington Atlas and Gazetteer:* Page 48 C4.

From the east (Yakima), drive west on Highway 410. The park boundary is 13.0 miles past the hamlet of American River. From the park boundary continue 3.6 miles west on Highway 410 and turn left (south) on Highway 123. Drive 11.2 miles, and turn right (west) onto Stevens Canyon Road; the entrance station is directly in front of you. *DeLorme: Washington Atlas and Gazetteer:* Page 48 C4.

Nisqually Entrance Station: From the north (Seattle or Tacoma), go south on I–5 to Highway 512, just south of Tacoma. Drive 2.0 miles east on Highway 512 and turn south onto Highway 7. Drive 31.0 miles south to Elbe and go east on Highway 706. Continue 13.0 miles to the park boundary. The last town before entering the park is Ashford, so be sure to stock up on supplies. The Nisqually Entrance Station is 5.0 miles east of Ashford. Once inside the Mount Rainier National Park, Highway 706 becomes the Longmire-Paradise Road. *DeLorme: Washington Atlas and Gazetteer:* Page 48 C1.

From the south (Portland), drive about 80.0 miles north on I–5 to US 12. Go 30.0 miles east on US 12, then turn north onto Highway 7. Drive 17.0 miles north to Elbe and turn east onto Highway 706. Drive 13.0 miles to the park boundary. The last town before entering the park is Ashford, so be sure to stock up on supplies. The Nisqually Entrance

Station is 5.0 miles east of Ashford. *DeLorme: Washington Atlas and Gazetteer:* Page 48 C1.

From the East (Yakima), drive west on US 12 to Highway 123. Turn right (north) onto Highway 123 and drive 3.0 miles to the park entrance. Turn left (west) onto Stevens Canyon Road. Pay the entrance fee at the Stevens Canyon Entrance Station and continue west on Stevens Canyon Road, which eventually becomes Longmire-Paradise Road. The Nisqually Entrance Station is 6.7 miles west of the Longmire Historic District. *DeLorme: Washington Atlas and Gazetteer:* Page 48 C1.

Carbon River Entrance Station: Whether you are coming from the north or south, the best route starts from Tacoma. From Tacoma go east on Highway 512 to Highway 410. Go about 16 miles east on Highway 410 to Highway 165 in the town of Buckley. Go right (south) on Highway 165 until you reach Wilkeson. Continue from Wilkeson for 9.0 miles to where the road forks. Go to the left (east) onto Carbon River Road. Continue 8.0 miles to the Carbon River Entrance Station. *DeLorme: Washington Atlas and Gazetteer:* Page 48 A1.

From the east (Yakima), drive west on Highway 410 to Buckley. The junction with Highway 165 is in the middle of Buckley. Turn left and drive south on Highway 165 until you reach Wilkeson. Continue 9.0 miles to where the road forks. Go to the left (east) onto Carbon River Road. Continue 8.0 miles to the Carbon River Entrance Station. *DeLorme: Washington Atlas and Gazetteer:* Page 48 A1.

White River Entrance Station: From the north (Seattle or Tacoma), go south on I-5 to Highway 512, which originates in Tacoma. Drive east on Highway 512 until you reach Highway 410. Go east on Highway 410, which starts going east and then bends south as it nears the park. The road enters Mount Rainier National Park and continues 4.5 miles to White River Road. Turn right (west) and go 1.5 miles to the White River Entrance Station. *DeLorme: Washington Atlas and Gazetteer:* Page 48 A4.

From the south (Portland), drive about 80 miles north on I-5 to US 12. Go 72.0 miles east on US 12 and turn left (north) onto Highway 123, 7.0 miles east of Packwood. Continue 14.2 miles north on Highway 123 and stay left (west) on Highway 410. Drive 1.9 miles and turn left (west) onto White River Road. Continue 1.5 miles to the White River Entrance Station. *DeLorme: Washington Atlas and Gazetteer:* Page 48 A4.

From the east (Yakima), drive west on Highway 410. The park boundary is 13.0 miles past the hamlet of American River. From the park boundary continue west on Highway 410 for 3.6 miles to the junction with Highway 123. Stay on Highway 410 to the right and drive 1.9 miles to White River Road. Turn left (west) onto White River Road and drive 1.5 miles to the White River Entrance Station. *DeLorme: Washington Atlas and Gazetteer:* Page 48 A4.

Here are a few services that provide transportation to and from Mount Rainier:

- **Rainier Overland:** Operates shuttles by reservation between Sea-Tac Airport and Ashford, as well as points within Mount Rainier National Park. Call for rates and reservations: (360) 569–0851.

- **Rainier Shuttle:** Operates shuttles by reservation between Sea-Tac Airport and Ashford, as well as points within Mount Rainier National Park. Call for rates and reservations: (360) 569–2331.

- **Grayline Bus Services:** Bus service from downtown Seattle. Call for rates and reservations: (800) 231–2222; (206) 628–5526.

Visitor Facilities

Ranger Stations

Paradise Climbing Ranger Station: (360) 569–2211, ext. 2314

The Paradise Climbing Ranger Station mainly issues climbing permits for routes starting from Paradise, but you can obtain Wilderness Camping Permits and information here as well. This ranger station is open mid-May to late September. From the Nisqually Entrance Station (see Getting There), drive 15.9 miles east on Longmire-Paradise Road to the intersection with Stevens Canyon Road. Stay to the left and head 2.2 miles up to the Paradise complex. From the Stevens Canyon Entrance Station (see Getting There), drive nearly 19 miles west on the Stevens Canyon Road to the intersection with the Longmire-Paradise Road. Turn right (north) and follow the signs to Paradise.

Mowich Ranger Station

The Mowich Ranger Station, located on the west side of Mowich Lake, does not issue permits or provide wilderness information. It does, however, serve as a location to pick up food caches along the Wonderland Trail. From Wilkeson drive 9.0 miles south on Highway 165 to where the road forks. Stay to the right (south) at this fork, the way to Mowich Lake. After 3.2 miles the road becomes a well-maintained dirt road, although it can be slippery when muddy. Follow this road for another 8.8 miles to the Paul Peak trailhead on the right (south) side of the road. Pause at the fee station here and pay the park entrance fee, then continue southeast 5.3 miles to Mowich Lake, a total of 26.3 miles from Wilkeson.

Sunrise Ranger Station: (360) 663–2425

The Sunrise Ranger Station is located in the Sunrise Complex and shares a phone number with the Sunrise Visitor Center. This facility does occasionally issue permits if someone is available, but your best bet is to stop at the White River Wilderness Information Center in order to obtain Wilderness Camping Permits. The Sunrise Ranger Station opens in early July, about the time the White River Road opens, and stays open throughout the summer. From the White River Entrance Station (see Getting There), drive 13.8 miles west on White River Road to the Sunrise complex.

Wilderness Information Centers

Longmire Wilderness Information Center: (360) 569–HIKE (4453)

Open late May to October, the Longmire Wilderness Information Center issues Wilderness Camping Permits primarily for backpacking. The center has rangers equipped to help with any questions you might have, as well as a large relief map of the park. The Longmire Wilderness Information Center is located in the Longmire Historic District, along Longmire-Paradise Road. From the Nisqually Entrance Station (see Getting There), drive 6.7 miles east to the Longmire Historic District.

White River Wilderness Information Center: (360) 569–6030

This center issues permits primarily for backpacking and north-side climbing routes. Open late May through summer, the White River Wilderness Information Center is located next to the White River Entrance Station (see Getting There).

Wilkeson Wilderness Information Center: (360) 829–5127

Staff issues permits primarily for backpacking and north-side climbing routes. This center opens mid-May and stays open until the end of September. Drive to Wilkeson on Highway 165. The Wilkeson Wilderness Information Center is located in the center of Wilkeson's quaint downtown strip at 569 Church Street.

Visitor Centers and Museums

Sunrise Visitor Center: (360) 663–2425

The Sunrise Visitor Center provides a wealth of historical and geological information about Mount Rainier National Park. It opens in early July, about the time the White River Road opens, and stays open throughout the summer. From the White River Entrance Station, drive 13.8 miles west on White River Road to the Sunrise Complex.

Ohanapecosh Visitor Center: (360) 569–6046

The Ohanapecosh Visitor Center provides a variety of exhibits and information about Mount Rainier National Park. In some cases you can also get permits at the Ohanapecosh Visitor Center, but plan on getting your permit from one of the main locations listed above. The visitor center usually opens after Memorial Day and stays open until Labor Day. From the Stevens Canyon Entrance Station (see Getting There), drive 1.8 miles south on Highway 123 to the turnoff for Ohanapecosh Campground. The road forks just after you turn in; go right (north) and drive until the Ohanapecosh Visitor Center appears directly in front of you.

Jackson Visitor Center: (360) 569–6036

The Jackson Visitor Center is located in the Paradise Complex and offers a variety of natural and cultural information through exhibits, guided walks, and nature talks. The visitor center is open year-round on the weekends, but usually opens daily after Memorial Day weekend until Labor Day weekend. From the Nisqually Entrance Station (see Getting There), drive 15.9 miles east on Longmire-Paradise Road to the intersection with Stevens Canyon Road. Stay to the left and head 2.2 miles up to the Paradise Complex. From the Stevens Canyon Entrance Station (see Getting There), drive nearly 19 miles west on the Stevens Canyon Road to the intersection with the Longmire-Paradise Road. Turn right (north) and follow the signs to Paradise.

Longmire Museum: (360) 569–2211, ext. 3314

The Longmire Museum offers a range of information, such as natural history, cultural history, backpacking, hiking, and trail conditions. It issues permits only when the Longmire Wilderness Information Center is closed. The Longmire Museum is located in the Longmire Historic District, along Longmire-Paradise Road. From the Nisqually Entrance Station (see Getting There), drive 6.7 miles east to the Longmire Historic District.

1 Skyline Trail

Quite possibly the most popular hike in Mount Rainier National Park, the Skyline Trail is very well maintained and partly paved, with a close-up view of the Nisqually Glacier.

Start: Skyline trailhead.
Distance: 5.2-mile loop.
Approximate hiking time: 2 to 3 hours.
Elevation gain: 1,400 feet.
Seasons: Mid-July through September.
Nearest towns: Ashford, Packwood.
Fees and permits: $10.00 vehicle or $5.00 individual entry fee (seven days); $30.00 annual entry fee. Wilderness Camping Permits free—reservations recommended ($20 fee).

Maps: USGS: Mount Rainier East; Trails Illustrated Mount Rainier National Park; Astronaut's Vista: Mount Rainier National Park, Washington; Earthwalk Press Hiking Map & Guide.
Trail contacts: Paradise Ranger Station, (360) 569-2211, ext. 2314.
Jackson Visitor Center—Paradise, (360) 569-6036.
Trail conditions: www.nps.gov/mora/trail/tr_cnd.htm; weather, www.nps.gov/mora/current/weather.htm.

Finding the trailhead: From the Nisqually Entrance Station (see Getting There), travel 16.0 miles east on Longmire-Paradise Road. Stay to the left (north) where the road forks, following the signs to Paradise. From the Stevens Canyon Entrance Station (see Getting There), travel nearly 19 miles on Stevens Canyon road to the intersection with Longmire-Paradise Road. Turn right (north) and follow the signs to Paradise. If possible, bypass the visitor center and park by the Paradise Ranger Station and the Paradise Inn. *DeLorme: Washington Atlas and Gazetteer:* Page 48 B2, B3.

Skyline Trail

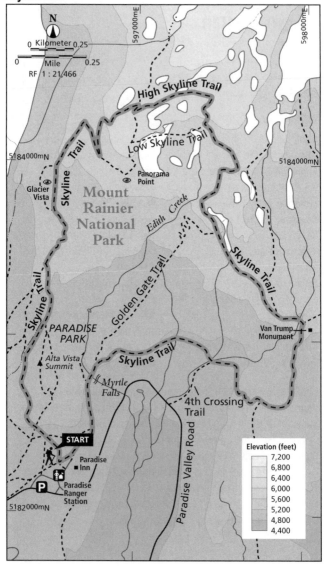

Special considerations: Parking at the Paradise Complex can get really hectic. Watch for a flashing sign when you enter the park that indicates whether the lots at Paradise are full, a common scenario on weekends from 11:00 A.M. until early evening. You can hope for a vacant spot, but if one does not open up promptly, consider an alternative hike.

The Hike

For good reason, more people visit Paradise than any other location on Mount Rainier. The views are spectacular, the services plentiful, and the trails many. Of all the trails in Paradise, Skyline is the most well known and frequently hiked. As you might guess by the name, the Skyline Trail goes above timberline into alpine terrain, with an awe-inspiring look at the Nisqually Glacier.

For the longest and best view of Mount Rainier, hike this trail clockwise. Start from the Skyline trailhead in the northwestern corner of the Paradise area parking lot. Rather than turning right (east), stay to the left (northwest), heading directly up the mountain. With so many intersecting trails, this area can get a bit confusing, but the Park Service has done a good job of putting up and maintaining clear, direct signposts that explicitly point the way. Stay on the Skyline Trail through all the intersections. You will likely see deer and marmots on this hike. Please do not feed the wildlife. They have already grown bold from constant handouts.

The trail ascends rather steeply for the next 2.0 miles, so prepare for a workout. At 1.1 miles, the Glacier Vista Trail intersects the main trail. For a slightly closer view of the Nisqually Glacier and a few words on the wonders of glaciation, take the Glacier Vista Trail to your left (west). It parallels the Skyline Trail briefly and then rejoins it. Back on the main trail, continue north for 0.5 mile of switchbacks, at which point the Low Skyline Trail splits to the right toward Panorama Point. Turn left (northeast) to stay on the High Skyline Trail.

Rocky alpine terrain provides the foreground for a remarkable view of Mount Rainier for nearly 0.5 mile. At the junction with the Pebble Creek Trail, 2.0 miles into the hike, you reach the top of your ascent. This is the path many mountaineers take on their trek to the summit. To see the Camp Muir Snowfield, turn left (north) onto the Pebble Creek Trail. A good glimpse of the path to the top can be had less than 0.5 mile from the turnoff, where Pebble Creek makes a good lunch spot.

Otherwise stay to the right (east), following the High Skyline Trail. You descend steeply along switchbacks in alpine terrain almost all the way to the Golden Gate Trail junction, about 0.8 mile. The Golden Gate Trail provides a shortcut back to Paradise, cutting about 2 miles off the hike length. To stay on the Skyline Trail, bear left.

In 0.7 mile a unique bench made of stone serves as a monument to P. B. Van Trump and Hazard Stevens, for the first recorded successful ascent of Mount Rainier. It also serves as a marker for the trailhead to the Paradise Glacier. Sit and relax on the stone slabs before continuing south on the Skyline Trail. Behind the monument, facing south, you have an excellent view of the Tatoosh Range on a sunny day.

Another 1.3 miles of descent with sporadic switchbacks lead to Myrtle Falls, a pretty little waterfall. You must walk to the bottom of the spur trail, a short side trip, to see it well. Return to the now-paved main trail. You should be able to see Paradise from the trail. Walk 0.4 mile back to the trailhead.

Miles and Directions

0.0   Start from the Skyline trailhead in the northwestern corner of the Paradise area parking lot. Stay to the left (northwest), heading directly up the mountain.

1.1   The Glacier Vista Trail spurs the main Skyline Trail, then rejoins just up the trail. Take the spur trail to see the display the park has erected on glaciation.

1.6   The Skyline Trail divides into the High and Low Skyline Trails. If the day is clear, take the Low Skyline Trail option to the right (southeast) and check out the vista at Panorama Point. Otherwise, go left (northeast) on the High Skyline Trail and see the Muir Snowfields and more alpine terrain.

2.0   Either way, in 0.4 mile you come upon Pebble Creek Trail. Stay on one of the Skyline Trails, which will converge in another 0.3 mile.

2.8   Unless you are in a time crunch, stay to the left (southeast) and remain on the Skyline Trail at the intersection with the Golden Gate Trail. If you need to shave a couple of miles off the hike, you can take the Golden Gate Trail back to Paradise.

3.4   Come to the Paradise Glacier Trail junction and, just beyond it, a surreal sort of rock loveseat in the trail known as the Van Trump Monument. Stay to the right (south) along the Skyline Trail.

4.8   Where the Golden Gate Trail rejoins the Skyline trail on your right, there is also a spur trail to Myrtle Falls on your left. Take this short jog on your left (south) for a quick look at the falls.

5.2   Welcome back to Paradise.

Option: If the day is clear, follow the Low Skyline Trail detour to Panorama Point. Less than 0.25 mile of good trail leads to an excellent viewpoint. Here a panoramic picture of the Tatoosh Range and other neighboring mountains is well labeled for your viewing pleasure and insight. A trail from Panorama Point joins the High Skyline Trail to the north, so you can easily jump back on the loop.

2 Rampart Ridge

One of the few hikes that are snow free in June, this short but steep hike up to Rampart Ridge affords you splendid views of Eagle Peak, Mount Rainier, and the Nisqually River Valley. The trail takes you through a quiet, dense forest to two viewpoints offering the possibility of seeing a variety of flora and fauna.

Start: Longmire Historic District.
Distance: 4.8-mile loop.
Approximate hiking time: 2 to 3 hours.
Elevation gain: 1,280 feet.
Seasons: June through September.
Nearest town: Ashford.
Fees and permits: $10.00 vehicle or $5.00 individual entry fee (seven days); $30.00 annual entry fee.

Maps: USGS: Mount Rainier West; Trails Illustrated Mount Rainier National Park; Astronaut's Vista: Mount Rainier National Park, Washington; Earthwalk Press Hiking Map & Guide.
Trail contacts: Longmire Wilderness Information Center, (360) 569-HIKE (4453).
Trail conditions: www.nps.gov/mora/trail/tr_cnd.htm; weather, www.nps.gov/mora/current/weather.htm.

Finding the trailhead: From Nisqually River Entrance Station (see Getting There), drive 6.7 miles east on the Longmire-Paradise Road to the Longmire Historic District. Turn right (southeast) into the parking lot around the Longmire Historic District, which includes Longmire

Rampart Ridge

Wonderland Trail

N

0   Kilometer   0.25

0   Mile   0.25
RF 1 : 19,250

5180000mN

590000mE

**Mount Rainier
National Park**

R   I   D   G   E

Elevation (feet)
| 4,200 |
| 3,900 |
| 3,600 |
| 3,300 |
| 3,000 |
| 2,700 |
| 2,400 |

R   A   M   P   A   R   T

Rampart Ridge Trail

T H E   R A M P A R T S

5179000mN

Spur
Trail

Wonderland Trail

Longmire-Paradise Road

Trail of the
Shadows
Nature Trail

Wonderland Trail

START

Longmire
Museum

Longmire Wilderness
Information Center

?

5178000mN

National Park Inn

P

Longmire
Historic
District

Longmire

Longmire
Community Building

590000mE

5178000mN

Wilderness Information Center, the Longmire Museum, and the National Park Inn. Walk on one of the two crosswalks across the Longmire-Paradise Road to the Rampart Ridge trailhead, located across the street from the inn. Finding a parking space at the Long-mire Historic District is a potential problem on sunny, summer week-ends. *DeLorme: Washington Atlas and Gazetteer:* Page 48 C2.

Special considerations: There are no water sources along this trail.

The Hike

This hike is great for people who like to climb hills, enjoy great scenery, and need a hike that is snow-free in June. In less than 2 miles the trail takes you up 1,200 feet and allows you to peer into the valley you just ventured from, as well as the valley on the other side of Rampart Ridge. The ridge itself, also known as the "Ramparts," is a remnant of ancient lava flow from Mount Rainier. The switchbacks are steep but definitely bearable. Remember to bring plenty of water, because this hike has no water sources.

Stay to your left (west) after crossing the street. A small section of the first part of the Rampart Ridge Trail is also part of the Trail of the Shadows, but the Rampart Ridge Trail veers off to the left after only 0.1 mile. The Trail of the Shadows (see Hike 5: Trail of the Shadows) is a self-guided hike that takes you around a field of mineral springs.

At the junction with the Rampart Ridge Trail, go right (north). For more than 1.5 miles there are relatively steep switchbacks, although they level out at the end just before the viewpoints. This part of the trail is mainly in the trees, but at one point you may catch a glimpse of Tumtum Peak to the west. After hiking 1.8 miles you reach a spur trail that goes to a viewpoint. Take a break and enjoy the scenery from the viewpoint. On a clear day you can see Eagle Peak, the Nisqually River, the Longmire Historic District, and Mount Rainier.

The next 1.2 miles along the ridge are flat and very pleasant. You can see down into the valley on the other side of Rampart Ridge along this section. A glimpse of Kautz Creek can be had 0.2 mile after the viewpoint. You arrive at the Wonderland Trail junction after traveling a little over a mile from the viewpoint. Go right (south) at this junction. This turn takes you off the Rampart Ridge Trail and onto the Wonderland Trail. From this point on, the trail loses elevation all the way back to the Longmire Historic District. About 0.2 mile after joining the Wonderland Trail, a trail leading to Van Trump Park splits off to the left (northeast). Stay to the right (south) here, and continue down the Wonderland Trail. At 4.6 miles cross Longmire-Paradise Road and continue hiking on the Wonderland Trail back to the Longmire Historic District. There are many signs to point the way on this last stretch.

Miles and Directions

0.0   Start at the Longmire Historic District. Hike across the Longmire-Paradise Road; stay to the left, heading west on the Trail of the Shadows until you reach the Rampart Ridge Trail.

0.1   At the junction with the Rampart Ridge Trail, go right (north).

1.8   A spur trail to the right goes to a viewpoint. Continue on the Rampart Ridge Trail, hiking northeast.

3.0   Arrive at the Wonderland Trail junction after traveling a little over a mile from the viewpoint. Go right (south) at this junction.

- **3.2** A trail that leads to Van Trump Park heads off to the left (northeast). Stay to the right, heading south.
- **4.6** Cross the Longmire-Paradise Road and continue hiking on the Wonderland Trail. There are many signs to point the way on this last stretch.
- **4.8** Arrive back at the Longmire Historic District.

3 Narada Falls

This completely downhill hike (with a vehicle shuttle) passes three waterfalls and runs through the scenic Paradise and Nisqually River Valleys.

Start: Narada Falls trailhead.
Distance: 4.5-mile shuttle.
Approximate hiking time: 2 to 3 hours.
Elevation loss: 2,044 feet.
Seasons: Early July through September.
Nearest town: Ashford.
Fees and permits: $10.00 vehicle or $5.00 individual entry fee (seven days); $30.00 annual entry fee. Wilderness Camping Permits free—reservations recommended ($20 fee).

Maps: USGS: Mount Rainier West and Mount Rainier East; Trails Illustrated Mount Rainier National Park; Astronaut's Vista: Mount Rainier National Park, Washington; Earthwalk Press Hiking Map & Guide.
Trail contacts: Longmire Wilderness Information Center, (360) 569–HIKE (4453).
Trail conditions: www.nps.gov/ mora/trail/tr_cnd.htm; weather, www.nps.gov/mora/current/ weather.htm.

Finding the trailhead: Hiking this trail one-way requires a short two-car shuttle. From the Nisqually Entrance Station (see Getting There), drive 6.7 miles east on Longmire-Paradise Road to the

Narada Falls

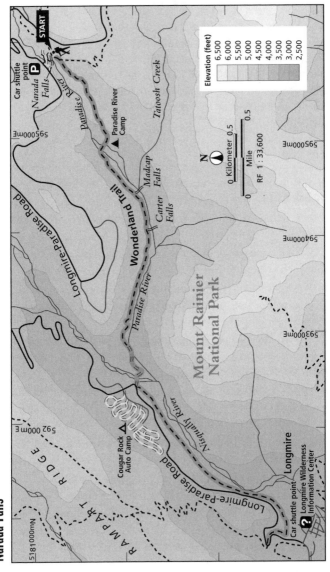

Elevation (feet)
- 6,500
- 6,000
- 5,500
- 5,000
- 4,500
- 4,000
- 3,500
- 3,000
- 2,500

START

Car shuttle point P
Narada Falls

595000mE

Longmire-Paradise Road

Paradise River

Paradise River Camp ▲

Madcap Falls

Carter Falls

Tatoosh Creek

Wonderland Trail

Paradise River

Mount Rainier National Park

594000mE

593000mE

N

0 Kilometer 0.5

0 Mile 0.5

RF 1 : 33,600

RAMPART RIDGE

592 000mE

Cougar Rock Auto Camp ▲

Nisqually River

Longmire-Paradise Road

Longmire

Car shuttle point
Longmire Wilderness Information Center ?

5181000mN

Longmire Historic District on the right (south). Park one car here. *DeLorme: Washington Atlas and Gazetteer:* Page 48 C2.

In the second vehicle continue roughly 8 miles east on Longmire-Paradise Road and turn right (east) into the parking lot signed for Narada Falls. The Narada Falls Trail is on the far east side of the parking lot before the restrooms. Park and walk over the bridge until you see the trailhead on the right (south). DeLorme: Washington Atlas and Gazetteer: Page 48 B2.

The Hike

This hike passes three waterfalls and travels all downhill. You begin at the astonishing Narada Falls and then hike by two other waterfalls, Madcap and Carter Falls. The only disadvantage of this hike is that it requires two vehicles. If you do not have access to two cars, consider starting at the Longmire Historic District and doing an out-and-back hike. Other options include arranging a shuttle pickup or leaving a bike at the end of the hike and having one person ride back to pick up the car.

From the Narada Falls parking lot, go down the stone steps of the Narada Falls Trail that run along the falls. Narada Falls is wondrous, and on a hot day the cool spray of the falls is very refreshing. Do be careful on the slippery rocks. The first 0.2 mile on the Narada Falls Trail is usually extremely crowded, considering how close the magnificent falls are to the road.

▶ **The Native American term** *narada* **translates as "uncontaminated."**

Fortunately the traffic nearly disappears when you join the Wonderland Trail. Go right and head west on the Wonderland Trail. You can hear the Paradise River flowing directly to your right, which you cross about 1.0 mile into your hike (about 0.1 mile past Paradise River Camp on the left).

Three bridges take you over the relatively calm forks of the Paradise River. About 0.5 mile from here you encounter Madcap Falls, where the Tatoosh Creek flows into the Paradise River. Instead of dropping straight down, Madcap Falls slope at a diagonal. The water gushes over the rocks to create a white wonder.

Soon after Madcap Falls you come to Carter Falls. A sign reaffirms that the gorgeous waters you see dropping straight down are in fact Carter Falls. You might come upon a number of people here, considering the proximity to Cougar Rock Campground.

The next 1.1 miles are a pleasant walk along the Paradise River, despite some metal drain pipes and power lines along the trail. When you are 2.8 miles into your hike, you come to another set of bridges that take you across the Nisqually River. The waters of the Nisqually are thick with "glacial flour," fine sediments deposited by active glaciers at the river's source. The wide Nisqually River Valley is scattered with debris and downed trees from previous floods.

After you cross the bridges, climb up to Longmire-Paradise Road. The Wonderland Trail continues left (west). There is a sign to help you continue on the Wonderland Trail to Longmire. In less than 0.25 mile, you come to another junction. The trail to your right (north) goes to Cougar Rock Campground; the trail left (south) goes to an old horse ford across the Nisqually River. Continue heading southwest on the Wonderland Trail through beautiful forest all the way to the Longmire Historic District.

▶ **The Nisqually Glacier moves at least 11 inches a day in winter and a minimum of 2 feet a day in early summer.**

Miles and Directions

0.0 Start at the Narada Falls trailhead. Hike down the trail past Narada Falls.

0.2 The Narada Falls Trail meets the Wonderland Trail. Turn right onto the Wonderland Trail, heading west.

0.9 A trail to Paradise River Camp heads to the left (south). Stay on the Wonderland Trail, traveling west.

1.5 Encounter Madcap Falls.

1.7 Arrive at Carter Falls.

2.8 A trail to Longmire-Paradise Road. Stay to the left, hiking west on the Wonderland Trail.

4.5 Arrive at Longmire Historic District.

Option: Start at the Paradise Complex instead of Narada Falls, making your trip 1.2 miles longer. This allows you to travel all the way from the Paradise Complex to the Longmire Historic District. Park one car at the Longmire Historic District, and park the other car at the Paradise Complex. To get to the Paradise Complex from the Longmire Historic District, drive 11.4 miles east on Longmire-Paradise Road. Park in the parking lot in front of the Paradise Ranger Station and the Paradise Inn. Walk to the Lakes trailhead, located in the southeast corner of the parking lot. Stay on the Lakes Trail for less than 0.6 mile until you intersect with the Narada Falls Trail. Go west on the Narada Falls Trail for a little over 0.1 mile, until you reach the Longmire–Paradise Road. After you cross the road, travel along the Narada Falls Trail for another 0.5 mile until you reach Narada Falls. At this point, refer to the above hike description.

4 Comet Falls

This hike takes you by Comet Falls, one of the tallest falls in the park, named for its similarity to a comet's tail.

Start: Van Trump Park trailhead (otherwise known as the Comet Falls trailhead).
Distance: 3.8-mile out-and-back.
Approximate hiking time: 2.5 to 4 hours.
Elevation gain: 2,160 feet.
Seasons: Mid-July through September.
Nearest town: Ashford.
Fees and permits: $10.00 vehicle or $5.00 individual entry fee (seven days); $30.00 annual entry fee.

Maps: USGS: Mount Rainier West; Trails Illustrated Mount Rainier National Park; Astronaut's Vista: Mount Rainier National Park, Washington; Earthwalk Press Hiking Map & Guide.
Trail contacts: Longmire Wilderness Information Center, (360) 569–HIKE (4453).
Trail conditions: www.nps.gov/mora/trail/tr_cnd.htm; weather, www.nps.gov/mora/current/weather.htm.

Finding the trailhead: From the Nisqually Entrance Station (see Getting There), drive 10.7 miles east on Longmire-Paradise Road. The parking lot is on your left, but it is often overcrowded on sunny weekends. If you cannot select a space in the parking lot or in the few spaces across the road, you might have to find an alternative hike. *DeLorme: Washington Atlas and Gazetteer:* Page 48 B2.

The Hike

The trail takes you through beautiful forest to several waterfalls, including Comet Falls, one of the tallest falls in the park.

Comet Falls

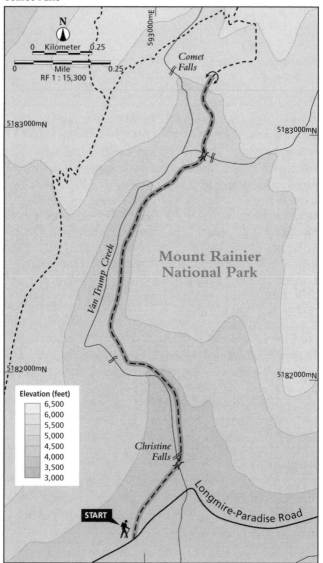

N

0 Kilometer 0.25

0 Mile 0.25
RF 1 : 15,300

5183000mN

5183000mN

Comet Falls

Van Trump Creek

Mount Rainier National Park

5182000mN

5182000mN

Elevation (feet)
6,500
6,000
5,500
5,000
4,500
4,000
3,500
3,000

Christine Falls

START

Longmire-Paradise Road

From the Van Trump Park Trail parking lot, travel north up the Van Trump Park Trail. In less than 0.3 mile you come to a bridge over the top of Christine Falls. The trail stays mainly in the forest all the way, but it opens up just before you view Comet Falls. At that point you can relish Van Trump Creek on your left and the bushes of salmonberries to your right.

You come to a bridge before you reach Comet Falls. The trail seems to fork before the bridge, but stay to the left (north). The trail to the right (east) is a small spur trail that wraps around the bend to the foot of an unnamed falls. You have a nice view of the falls from the bridge.

When you reach your first view of Comet Falls, 1.7 miles from the beginning of your hike, several viewing areas await. The white waters of Comet Falls resemble the tail of a comet, the inspiration for its name. The spectacular falls are visible from the bottom of the switchbacks, but you have to travel 0.2 mile up the steep switchbacks adjacent to the falls to receive a close-up, and likely wet, view.

Miles and Directions

0.0 Start at the Van Trump Park trailhead (sometimes referred to as Comet Falls trailhead). Travel north up the Van Trump Park Trail.

1.9 You reach Comet Falls, but there are numerous viewing opportunities before you actually reach the falls. Enjoy the falls before retracing your steps.

3.8 Arrive back at the trailhead.

5 Trail of the Shadows

A thirty-minute stroll around the Longmire Meadow, with attractions that inform you about the Longmire family and its stake in the park.

Start: Longmire Historic District.
Distance: 0.7-mile lollipop.
Approximate hiking time: 30 minutes.
Elevation gain: Minimal.
Seasons: May through October.
Nearest town: Ashford.
Fees and permits: $10.00 vehicle or $5.00 individual entry fee (seven days); $30.00 annual entry fee.

Maps: USGS: Mount Rainier West; Trails Illustrated Mount Rainier National Park; Astronaut's Vista: Mount Rainier National Park, Washington; Earthwalk Press Hiking Map & Guide.
Trail contacts: Longmire Wilderness Information Center, (360) 569–HIKE (4453).
Trail conditions: www.nps.gov/ mora/trail/tr_cnd.htm; weather, www.nps.gov/mora/current/ weather.htm.

Finding the trailhead: From the Nisqually Entrance Station (see Getting There), drive 6.7 miles east on Longmire-Paradise Road. Look for the Longmire Historic District on the right (east). Park in one of the many spaces around the Longmire Wilderness Information Center, the Longmire Museum, and the National Park Inn, then cross the road along one of the two crosswalks to find the trailhead. *DeLorme: Washington Atlas and Gazetteer:* Page 48 C2.

The Hike

If you are a history buff who likes casual strolls, you will enjoy this hike. The trail winds around an enchanting meadow, while taking you to many informative stations. The

Trail of the Shadows

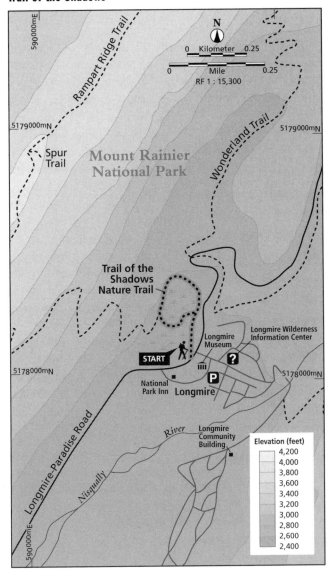

theme of the stations is James Longmire, his crusade for a natural health spa, and his love of the mountain.

Starting to the right (north), the first stop is a work of stone masonry with bubbling water, said in the nineteenth century to cure any illness. As the sign ironically reads, DO NOT DRINK THIS WATER; IT CAN MAKE YOU VERY ILL.

► In 1870 James Longmire brought P. B. Van Trump and Hazard Stevens to Sluiskin, a Native American guide, and persuaded Sluiskin to guide Van Trump and Stevens on the first well-documented ascent to the summit. After securing a guide, James Longmire returned to his farm.

The next stop, 0.2 mile into the hike, is the cabin that Longmire built. It still has the original furniture, also constructed by Longmire. Next door is Iron Mike, a spring that is tinted orange by iron minerals.

A very small side trip at 0.5 mile from the trailhead leads to the Travertine Mound, another orange mass bursting with mineral water. A bench here provides a nice place to sit and view the meadow.

The home stretch of the loop includes a variety of interesting wild vegetation. After completing the loop, cross the Longmire-Paradise Road again to get back to your car and the large present-day Longmire Historic District. Notice the great disparity between the present-day edifices and the shadows of the past.

Miles and Directions

0.0 Start at the Longmire Historic District. Cross the road along one of the two crosswalks to find the trailhead.

0.1 You're standing before the masonry spring.

0.2 Pass Longmire's cabin.

0.2 Reach Iron Mike.

0.5 A small spur trail takes you to the Travertine Mound.

0.7 Return to the trailhead. Head back across the road to the Longmire Historic District.

6 Alta Vista Summit

This short hike travels through beautiful forest overlooking the Nisqually Glacier.

Start: Jackson Visitor Center.
Distance: 1.6-mile lollipop.
Approximate hiking time: 1 hour.
Elevation gain: Minimal.
Seasons: Early July through September.
Nearest towns: Ashford, Packwood.
Fees and permits: $10.00 vehicle or $5.00 individual entry fee (seven days); $30.00 annual entry fee.
Maps: USGS: Mount Rainier East; Trails Illustrated Mount

Rainier National Park; Astronaut's Vista: Mount Rainier National Park, Washington; Earthwalk Press Hiking Map & Guide.
Trail contacts: Paradise Ranger Station, (360) 569-2211 ext. 2314.
Jackson Visitor Center–Paradise, (360) 569-6036.
Trail conditions: www.nps.gov/ mora/trail/tr_cnd.htm; weather, www.nps.gov/mora/current/ weather.htm.

Finding the trailhead: From the Nisqually Entrance Station (see Getting There), travel 16.0 miles east on Longmire-Paradise Road. Stay to the left (north) where the road forks, following the signs to Paradise. From the Stevens Canyon Entrance Station (see Getting There), travel nearly 19 miles on Stevens Canyon Road to the intersection with Longmire-Paradise Road. Turn right (north) and follow the signs to Paradise. Park in the lot by the Jackson Visitor Center, if possible. *DeLorme: Washington Atlas and Gazetteer:* Page 48 B2, B3.

Alta Vista Summit

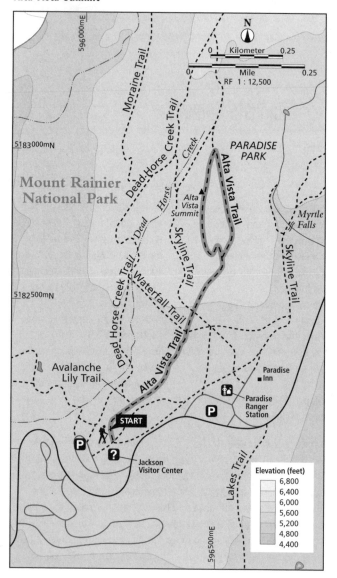

Special considerations: Parking at the Paradise Complex can get really hectic. Watch for a flashing sign when you enter the park that indicates whether the parking lots at Paradise are full, a common scenario on weekends from 11:00 A.M. until early evening. You can hope for a vacant spot, but if one does not open up promptly, consider an alternative hike.

The Hike

This hike is excellent for children. It is short and scenic and gives you a little taste of Mount Rainier National Park. If you take this hike in July or August, an abundance of wildflowers will line the trails. Please preserve the fragile meadows where the flowers grow by staying on the trail. Expect to see a lot of people on this popular trail.

The trail, paved and well maintained, begins directly west of the Jackson Visitor Center. No trailhead sign marks the beginning of the Alta Vista Trail, but follow the paved steps that head north for just a few steps and you will come to a display of trails in the Paradise area. Do not take the spur trail heading to the right (east); it leads to the Paradise Ranger Station.

Continue 0.1 mile north on the Alta Vista Trail to the Avalanche Lily Trail, which runs west to the Dead Horse Creek Trail and east to the Paradise Ranger Station. Go straight and immediately pass another small spur trail that connects with the Avalanche Lily Trail on your left, heading southwest. Stay on the Alta Vista Trail, traveling north. There are detailed signs to help you continue on the Alta Vista Trail.

After another 0.1 mile the Waterfall Trail goes left (west) to connect with the Dead Horse Creek Trail or right (east) to the Skyline Trail. Again, stay on the Alta Vista Trail, heading north. Very soon after this junction, you come to the Skyline

Trail. Again, stay on the Alta Vista Trail. At this point the trail grade turns markedly steep. Pace yourself.

About 0.5 mile into your hike, you come to the beginning of the loop to the Alta Vista summit. Go left (northwest) and uphill toward the summit with the help of a sign that points you in the correct direction. Below, Paradise Park is to the right (east). You can see tons of people milling about below you on other Paradise trails. Turn around and look to the south for a fabulous view of the jutting peaks of the Tatoosh Range.

If you need a rest, enjoy the view from one of the many rock benches along the trail. Please preserve the meadows by staying on the trail or in a designated rest area.

When you have enjoyed yourself to the fullest, complete the loop by continuing north on the Alta Vista Trail, or simply turn around and go back the way you came. If you decide to complete the loop, you reach the east side of the loop 0.1 mile from the summit, about 0.8 mile from the Jackson Visitor Center. Turn right and head south on the east side of the Alta Vista Trail until the loop rejoins itself, 1.1 miles into your hike. From this point, head back down the trail to the parking lot.

Miles and Directions

0.0 Start heading directly west of the Jackson Visitor Center. No trailhead sign marks the beginning of the Alta Vista Trail; follow the paved steps that head north for just a few steps and you will come to a display of trails.

0.1 At the junction with the Avalanche Lily Trail, which heads toward the Dead Horse Creek Trail to the west and Paradise ranger station to the right, stay straight ahead on the Alta Vista Trail.

- **0.2** Again, stay on the Alta Vista Trail, heading north when the Waterfall Trail crosses your path.
- **0.5** The loop of the lollipop begins. Take a left (west) at the fork, following the signs for Alta Vista Summit. Notice Paradise Park down below you to the northeast and the myriad hikers on other trails in the area.
- **1.1** Complete the loop; stay to the left (south) at the stem of the lollipop.
- **1.6** Reach the Jackson Visitor Center and the parking lot where you most likely left your car.

7 Nisqually Vista

This short hike travels through beautiful forest overlooking the Nisqually Glacier.

Start: Deadhorse Creek trailhead.
Distance: 1.2-mile lollipop.
Approximate hiking time: 1 hour.
Elevation gain: Minimal.
Seasons: Early July through September.
Nearest town: Ashford, Packwood.
Fees and permits: $10.00 vehicle or $5.00 individual entry fee (seven days); $30.00 annual entry fee.

Maps: USGS: Mount Rainier East; Trails Illustrated Mount Rainier National Park; Astronaut's Vista: Mount Rainier National Park, Washington; Earthwalk Press Hiking Map & Guide.
Trail contacts: Paradise Ranger Station, (360) 569-2211, ext. 2314; Jackson Visitor Center—Paradise, (360) 569-6036.
Trail conditions: www.nps.gov/mora/trail/tr_cnd.htm; weather, www.nps.gov/mora/current/weather.htm.

Nisqually Vista

N

Kilometer
0   0.2

Mile
0   0.2

RF 1 : 10,900

Elevation (feet)

| 6,000 |
| 5,600 |
| 5,200 |
| 4,800 |
| 4,400 |
| 4,000 |

PARADISE PARK

Nisqually Vista Trail

Nisqually Vista

START

Dead Horse Creek

Dead Horse Creek Trail

Avalanche Lily Trail

Alta Vista Trail

Waterfall Trail

Skyline Trail

Paradise Inn

Paradise Ranger Station

Jackson Visitor Center

Mount Rainier National Park

595500mE

596000mE

596000mE

5182000mN

5182000mN

5183000mN

Finding the trailhead: From the Nisqually Entrance Station (see Getting There), travel 16 miles east on Longmire-Paradise Road. Stay to the left (north) where the road forks, following the signs to Paradise. From the Stevens Canyon Entrance Station (see Getting There), travel nearly 19 miles on Stevens Canyon Road to the intersection with Longmire-Paradise Road. Turn right (north) and follow the signs to Paradise. Park in the lot by the Jackson Visitor Center, if possible. *DeLorme: Washington Atlas and Gazetteer: Page 48 B2, B3.*

Special considerations: Parking at the Paradise Complex can get really hectic. Watch for a flashing sign when you enter the park that indicates whether the parking lots at Paradise are full, a common scenario on weekends from 11:00 A.M. until early evening. You can hope for a vacant spot, but if one does not open up promptly, consider an alternative hike.

The Hike

This is a great hike for kids and adults alike. The trail takes you through beautiful forested areas and wonderful meadows to an overlook of the Nisqually Glacier. The Nisqually Vista Trail is a self-guiding trail, but the National Park Service offers a guided tour of this hike in summer and leads snowshoe walks throughout winter. Inquire at the Jackson Visitor Center for more information. It is downhill all the way to the lookout and then uphill back to the parking lot, but both gradients are gradual.

To begin the hike, head to the northwest end of the Jackson Visitor Center parking lot. Look for a trail sign for the Dead Horse Creek Trail. Stay toward the left (northwest), and take the Nisqually Vista Trail, which branches off very near the inception of the hike. In less than 0.3 mile the trail forks again. This fork marks the beginning of the loop section of this lollipop. You could go either way. We recommend heading left (west) on the Nisqually Vista Trail. Halfway through the loop, and halfway through your hike, you come to a viewpoint. There are three viewpoints, and the first one has a display on the Nisqually Glacier.

From all the viewpoints you can see where the Nisqually River originates from the Nisqually Glacier and the massive moraine kicked up by years of glacial movement. The Nisqually Glacier is a relatively active one. Once it extended all the way to Ricksecker Point. You might have seen Ricksecker Point on the way from Longmire to Paradise. The point is visible from the only bridge between the two areas.

The rest of the loop is a little over 0.3 mile long and takes you through quaint forest with meadows of lupine and pasqueflower (commonly called bottlebrush). When you come to the end of the loop, stay to the left, toward the visitor center. Enjoy a leisurely hike back to the parking lot.

Miles and Directions

0.0 Start heading to the northwest end of the Jackson Visitor Center parking lot. Look for a trail sign for the Dead Horse Creek Trail. Stay toward the left (northwest), and take the Nisqually Vista Trail, which branches off very near the inception of the hike.

0.3 Nisqually Vista Trail forks at the loop part of the lollipop trail. Stay to the left (west), following the Nisqually Vista Trail.

0.6 Halfway through the hike, come to the first viewpoint of the Nisqually Glacier, the Nisqually River, and the moraine; the viewpoint provides an informational display. Two more viewpoints follow in quick succession.

0.9 End of loop; stay to the left (east) on the Nisqually Vista Trail.

1.2 At the Dead Horse Creek trailhead, the hike is basically over; you can see the parking lot of the Jackson Visitor Center.

8 Dead Horse Creek

This short spur trail connects with the Skyline Trail and has great views of the Tatoosh Range, Mount Rainier, and the Nisqually Glacier.

Start: Jackson Visitor Center parking lot.
Distance: 2.2-mile out-and-back.
Approximate hiking time: 1 hour.
Elevation gain: 600 feet.
Seasons: July through September.
Nearest towns: Ashford, Packwood.
Fees and permits: $10.00 vehicle or $5.00 individual entry fee (seven days); $30.00 annual entry fee. Wilderness Camping Permits free—reservations recommended ($20 fee).

Maps: USGS: Mount Rainier East; Trails Illustrated Mount Rainier National Park; Astronaut's Vista: Mount Rainier National Park, Washington; Earthwalk Press Hiking Map & Guide.
Trail contacts: Paradise Ranger Station, (360) 569-2211 ext. 2314. Jackson Visitor Center–Paradise, (360) 569-6036.
Trail conditions: www.nps.gov/mora/trail/tr_cnd.htm; weather, www.nps.gov/mora/current/weather.htm.

Finding the trailhead: From the Nisqually Entrance Station (see Getting There), drive nearly 16 miles east on Longmire-Paradise Road to the turnoff for the Ohanapecosh area. Stay to the left and continue on Longmire-Paradise Road for 2.1 miles. From the Stevens Canyon Entrance Station (see Getting There), travel nearly 19 miles on Stevens Canyon Road to the intersection with Longmire-Paradise Road. Turn right (north) and follow the signs to Paradise. If possible, park in the parking lot in front of the Jackson Visitor Center. *DeLorme: Washington Atlas and Gazetteer:* Page 48 B2, B3.

Special considerations: Parking at the Paradise Complex can get really hectic. Watch for a flashing sign when you enter the park that

Dead Horse Creek

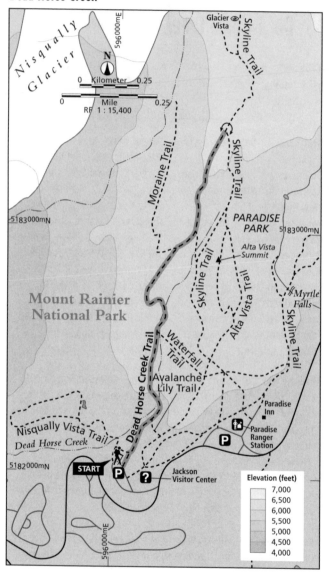

Glacier Vista

Skyline Trail

Nisqually Glacier

N

Kilometer
0   0.25

Mile
0   0.25
RF 1 : 15,400

Moraine Trail

Skyline Trail

PARADISE PARK

5183000mN

Alta Vista Summit

Skyline Trail

Alta Vista Trail

Myrtle Falls

Mount Rainier National Park

Skyline Trail

Waterfall Trail

Avalanche Lily Trail

Dead Horse Creek Trail

Paradise Inn

Paradise Ranger Station

Nisqually Vista Trail

Dead Horse Creek

START

P

?

Jackson Visitor Center

5182000mN

596000mE

596000mE

Elevation (feet)	
	7,000
	6,500
	6,000
	5,500
	5,000
	4,500
	4,000

indicates whether the parking lots at Paradise are full. Even if all the lots are not full, the lot in front of the visitor center is likely to be full. If it is, you can drive another 0.1 mile up the road to the parking lot in front of the Paradise Ranger Station and the Paradise Inn.

The Hike

If you want to hike the Skyline Trail but would prefer a shorter, more gradual ascent, consider the Dead Horse Creek Trail as an alternative. In August, wildflowers, including lupine and Lewis monkeyflower, line your path. Please preserve these flowers by staying on designated trails.

To start the hike, head to the west end of the parking lot. Look for a trail sign for the Dead Horse Creek Trail. Stay to the right, heading north on the Dead Horse Creek Trail. The trail first takes you through serene subalpine forest. Although the Paradise area is extremely high traffic, this trail receives less use than others in the area.

Wildlife is commonly seen along the trail. Deer, grouse, and marmots often venture into this area. Remember not to feed these wild animals; they need to remain self-sufficient to survive in their natural habitat. Also, it is illegal to feed the wildlife in Mount Rainier National Park.

Continue going north on the Dead Horse Creek Trail, ignoring the two trails that come in from the right at 0.1 mile (the Avalanche Lily Trail) and 0.4 mile (the Waterfall Trail). Both of these trails travel to the Paradise Ranger Station and the Paradise Inn. At every intersection a sign bears directions to help you stay on the Dead Horse Creek Trail. The Nisqually Glacier lies to the west. The National Park Service has set up several rock benches to help you enjoy this view. Please use the provided benches to minimize your impact on the fragile subalpine meadows.

The Moraine Trail intersects the Dead Horse Creek Trail from the left at 0.7 mile. Stay to the right (northeast), unless you plan to take the Moraine Trail option. Not far from the junction with the Moraine Trail, a small spur trail branches off to the right, connecting with the Skyline Trail. Stay on the main trail.

The trail is considerably steeper at this point, but you have only 0.4 mile to the end of the trail, over a mile into your hike. The end of Dead Horse Creek Trail is the Skyline Trail. You have the option of hiking back down the way you just came or making a loop by following the Skyline Trail. If you choose to take the Skyline Trail, follow the signs for it until you see a sign for the visitor center; follow the signs to the visitor center.

Miles and Directions

0.0 Start by heading to the west end of the Jackson Visitor Center parking lot. Look for a trail sign for the Dead Horse Creek Trail and stay to the right, heading north.

0.1 When the Avalanche Lily Trail comes in from the right (east), continue straight (north) on the Dead Horse Creek Trail.

0.4 Ignore the junction with the Waterfall Trail, which heads toward the Paradise Inn, and hike north on the Dead Horse Creek Trail.

0.7 The Moraine Trail spurs off to the left. If you want to see the Nisqually Glacier up-close and personal, you can take this option and add a mile of trail to your hiking time. Otherwise, stay to the right (northeast) along the Dead Horse Creek Trail. Also stay on the main trail when encountered with the connector to the Skyline Trail in just a few paces.

1.1 The Skyline Trail junction marks the end of the Dead Horse Creek Trail. You can turn around (south) or take a right (southeast) and follow signs to the visitor center.

2.2 Arrive back at the visitor center.

Option: More than halfway up the Dead Horse Creek Trail is the Moraine Trail. The park maintains this trail for less than 0.1 mile of its total 0.5-mile length. Taking this option adds 1.0 mile to your trip. The trail takes you down to the Nisqually Glacier Moraine, where the Nisqually River flows from its glacial source. People often hear and see chunks of ice falling from the end of the glacier. Be forewarned—the Moraine Trail is extremely steep.

9 High Lakes Trail

This short loop offers a great view of the Tatoosh Range and Reflection Lakes.

Start: Reflection Lakes.
Distance: 2.7-mile loop.
Approximate hiking time: 1 to 1.5 hours.
Elevation gain: Minimal.
Seasons: July through September.
Nearest towns: Ashford, Packwood.
Fees and permits: $10.00 vehicle or $5.00 individual entry fee (seven days); $30.00 annual entry fee. Wilderness Camping Permits free—reservations recommended ($20 fee).

Maps: USGS: Mount Rainier East; Trails Illustrated Mount Rainier National Park; Astronaut's Vista: Mount Rainier National Park, Washington; Earthwalk Press Hiking Map & Guide.
Trail contacts: Paradise Ranger Station, (360) 569-2211, ext. 2314.
Jackson Visitor Center–Paradise, (360) 569-6036.
Trail conditions: www.nps.gov/ mora/trail/tr_cnd.htm; weather, www.nps.gov/mora/current/ weather.htm.

High Lakes Trail

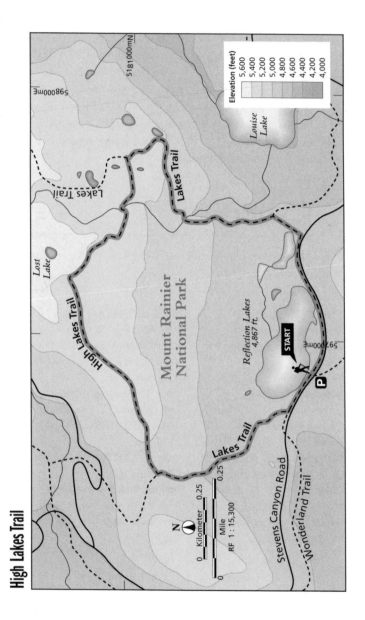

Mount Rainier National Park

High Lakes Trail

Lakes Trail

Lakes Trail

Lakes Trail

Lost Lake

Louise Lake

Reflection Lakes
4,867 ft.

START

P

Stevens Canyon Road

Wonderland Trail

5181000mN

5980000mE

5977000mE

Elevation (feet)

5,600
5,400
5,200
5,000
4,800
4,600
4,400
4,200
4,000

N

Kilometer   0.25

0

Mile   0.25

0   0.25

RF 1 : 15,300

Finding the trailhead: From Stevens Canyon Entrance Station (see Getting There), drive nearly 18 miles on Stevens Canyon Road to Reflection Lakes. From the Nisqually Entrance Station (see Getting There), travel nearly 16 miles east on Longmire-Paradise Road to the turnoff for the Ohanapecosh area. Turn right (southeast) onto Stevens Canyon Road and toward Ohanapecosh. Stay on this road for just under a mile. Reflection Lakes has three parking lots. The High Lakes Trail starts from the center parking lot, though you can access the trail from the flanking parking lots as well. The trail loops the lakes. *DeLorme: Washington Atlas and Gazetteer: Page 48 B3.*

The Hike

This is an easy day hike that explores the area around Reflection Lakes, possibly the most photographed spot on Mount Rainier. Aptly named, on a clear day you can see the entire mountain mirrored in the still waters of Reflection Lakes. The High Lakes Trail leaves the lakeside and follows Mazama Ridge, gaining just enough elevation to afford a view of the Tatoosh Range.

We recommend hiking this loop counterclockwise to lessen the elevation gain, but that decision is yours alone. From the Reflection Lakes parking lot, walk east along Stevens Canyon Road until you reach the junction with the Wonderland Trail toward Louise Lake. Go left (northeast) onto the Lakes Trail, leaving the Wonderland Trail behind. Continue on the Lakes Trail up the south side of Mazama Ridge—a relatively steep but short section—to the High Lakes Trail, 0.7 mile into your hike.

Turn left (west) onto the High Lakes Trail. This trail is mostly downhill or flat, with many opportunities to view the Tatoosh Range and three of its jagged pinnacles—Pinnacle, Plummer, and Unicorn Peaks—jutting above the horizon.

After 1.2 miles the High Lakes Trail rejoins the Lakes Trail. Go left (south) and downhill on the lower Lakes Trail for 0.5 mile to a junction with the Wonderland Trail. Stay to the left and head toward Reflection Lakes for the next 0.2 mile to Stevens Canyon Road. Walk 0.1 mile east along the road back to where you parked.

Miles and Directions

0.0 Start from the Reflection Lakes parking lot. Walk east along Stevens Canyon Road until you reach the junction with the Wonderland Trail toward Louise Lake.

0.3 The Wonderland Trail diverges from the Lakes Trail to head toward Louise Lake. Stay left (north) on the Lakes Trail and head up Mazama Ridge.

0.7 At the High Lakes Trail junction, make sure you take a left (west) onto High Lakes. Otherwise, you could follow the Lakes Trail all the way to Paradise.

1.9 When you reach the Lakes Trail junction, you have completed the top section of the loop known as the High Lakes Trail. Stay to the left (south) on the Lakes Trail to get back to your car.

2.4 Once again, the Wonderland Trail intersects the Lakes Trail. Stay to the left (southeast) toward the Reflection Lakes parking lot.

2.7 Arrive back at the Reflection Lakes trailhead.

10 Pinnacle Peak Saddle

A short climb up to the saddle between Pinnacle and Plummer Peaks offers great views of Mount Rainier along the trail and from the saddle.

Start: Pinnacle Peak trailhead, across from Reflection Lakes.
Distance: 2.6-mile out-and-back.
Approximate hiking time: 1 to 1.5 hours.
Elevation gain: 970 feet.
Seasons: Late July through September.
Nearest towns: Ashford, Packwood.
Fees and permits: $10.00 vehicle or $5.00 individual entry fee (seven days); $30.00 annual entry fee. Wilderness Camping Permits free—reservations recommended ($20 fee).

Maps: USGS: Mount Rainier East; Trails Illustrated Mount Rainier National Park; Astronaut's Vista: Mount Rainier National Park, Washington; Earthwalk Press Hiking Map & Guide.
Trail contacts: Paradise Ranger Station, (360) 569–2211 ext. 2314.
Jackson Visitor Center—Paradise, (360) 569-6036.
Trail conditions: www.nps.gov/mora/trail/tr_cnd.htm; weather, www.nps.gov/mora/current/weather.htm.

Finding the trailhead: From Stevens Canyon Entrance Station (see Getting There), drive nearly 18 miles on Stevens Canyon Road to Reflection Lakes. From the Nisqually Entrance Station (see Getting There), travel nearly 16 miles east on Longmire-Paradise Road to the turnoff for the Ohanapecosh area. Turn right (southeast) onto Stevens Canyon Road and toward Ohanapecosh. Stay on this road for just under a mile. Reflection Lakes has three parking lots. The well-marked trailhead to Pinnacle Peak starts opposite the middle lot. *DeLorme: Washington Atlas and Gazetteer:* Page 48 B3.

Pinnacle Peak Saddle

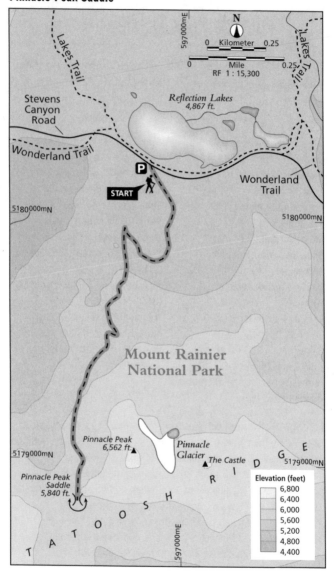

The Hike

This hike is uphill all the way to the turnaround point. Wild-flowers, such as lupine and magenta paintbrush, often grow along the trail in July and August. Pikas inhabit the rockfields along the trail, squeaking at passersby. The saddle offers an excellent view of Mount Rainier. Hope for a clear day.

There are no tricky turns or trail junctions on this hike. Simply start from the trailhead, directly across from the west end of Reflection Lakes, and hike all the way to the saddle. The first half of the trail is in the forest and climbs gradually, but once you hit the first rockfield, the trail becomes steep and rocky. Snow lingers on these rockfields late into summer—sturdy hiking boots are the footwear of choice here.

Once you reach the saddle, you can see to the south boundary of the park and all the way to Packwood. Plummer Peak rises to the right (west) and Pinnacle Peak to the left (east). Looking southeast you can see both Unicorn Peak and the Castle; to the southwest, Wahpenayo Peak is visible. Enjoy the amazing view before heading back the way you came.

Miles and Directions

0.0 Start heading south from the Pinnacle Peak trailhead, across Stevens Canyon Road from Reflection Lakes.

1.3 Reach the Pinnacle Peak saddle. Head back the way you came, or opt for the scramble to the top.

2.6 Arrive back at the trailhead.

Option: The maintained trail ends 1.3 miles into the hike, but there are unmaintained trails heading along the ridges of both Pinnacle and Plummer Peaks. The scramble up to Pinnacle Peak does not require technical climbing equipment, but it is hazardous and should be approached with caution.

11 Paradise Glacier

A short day hike over a snowfield brings you to the foot of a small glacier.

Start: Skyline trailhead.

Distance: 6.4-mile out-and-back.

Approximate hiking time: 3 to 4 hours.

Elevation gain: 1,000 feet.

Seasons: Mid-July through September.

Nearest towns: Ashford, Packwood.

Fees and permits: $10.00 vehicle or $5.00 individual entry fee (seven days); $30.00 annual entry fee. Wilderness Camping Permits free—reservations recommended ($20 fee).

Maps: USGS: Mount Rainier East; Trails Illustrated Mount Rainier National Park; Astronaut's Vista: Mount Rainier National Park, Washington; Earthwalk Press Hiking Map & Guide.

Trail contacts: Paradise Ranger Station, (360) 569-2211, ext. 2314.

Jackson Visitor Center–Paradise, (360) 569-6036.

Trail conditions: www.nps.gov/mora/trail/tr_cnd.htm; weather, www.nps.gov/mora/current/weather.htm.

Finding the trailhead: From the Nisqually Entrance Station (see Getting There), travel 16 miles east on Longmire-Paradise Road. Stay to the left (north) where the road forks, following the signs to Paradise. From the Stevens Canyon Entrance Station (see Getting There), travel nearly 19 miles on Stevens Canyon Road to the intersection with Longmire-Paradise Road. Turn right (north) and follow the signs to Paradise. If possible, bypass the visitor center and park by the Paradise Ranger Station and the Paradise Inn. *DeLorme: Washington Atlas and Gazetteer: Page 48 B2, B3.*

Special considerations: Parking at the Paradise Complex can get really hectic. Watch for a flashing sign when you enter the park that indi-

Paradise Glacier

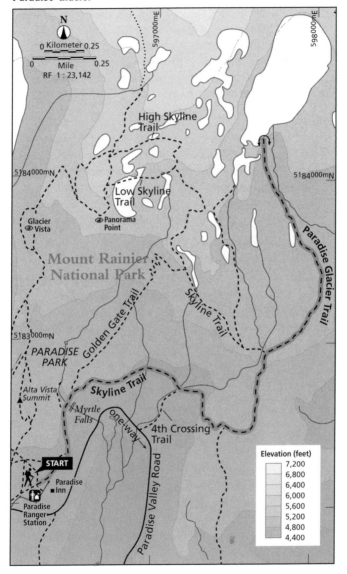

cates whether the lots at Paradise are full, a common scenario on weekends from 11:00 A.M. until early evening. You can hope for a vacant spot, but if one does not open up promptly, consider an alternative hike.

The Paradise Glacier Trail is no longer maintained by the Park Service, but crews do check on the cairns once a year. Do not expect an immaculate trail beyond the Skyline Trail.

The Hike

The ice caves that once drew many to this trail have melted with the general increase in global temperature. This means a less sensational hike, but it also means fewer passersby and the same spectacular view as before.

Start hiking along the Skyline Trail in the northwestern corner of the parking lot; the trailhead is well marked. Proceed to the right (east), counterclockwise along the loop. Many trails congest this area, but just follow the Skyline Trail signs eastbound and you will reach your destination.

Hike gradually uphill along a wide, paved trail for 0.4 mile to arrive at Myrtle Falls. The path to the bottom of the falls is short but steep and offers a closer look. Back on the main trail, cross Edith Creek, the source of Myrtle Falls; stay to the right beyond the Golden Gate Trail junction.

Climb steadily, through occasional switchbacks, for 0.3 mile to the 4th Crossing Trail. Stay to the left, continuing east. Much like previous parts of the trail, this is a medium ascent through subalpine forest. You soon reach the Lakes Trail junction, 1.4 miles into the hike. Again, stay to the left, heading northeast.

The trail turns to head north; 0.4 mile after the Lakes Trail junction, look for a stone bench at a fork in the trail. This firm resting spot was erected by the Mountaineers and the Mazamas as a tribute to Hazard Stevens and Philemon

Beecher Van Trump. The monument marks the campsite from which the two made the first recorded ascent of Mount Rainier. It also marks the Paradise Glacier Trail junction.

Turn right (east) onto the Paradise Glacier Trail. From here the ascent is gradual, but it leads into alpine terrain. Even in late summer expect to encounter quite a bit of snow; wear boots if you have them. The trail ends in a snowfield—hike only as far as you feel comfortable. No sign marks the end of the maintained trail. Cairns guide you to the snowfield, where the ice caves once were.

A good view of the Paradise Glacier is not the only reason to hike this trail. The snowfield, however, is a good place to play "name that glacier." Facing north up the trail, you have a close view of the glaciated mountain. To the east are the headwaters of Stevens Creek, and directly behind you (south) is an amazing view of the Tatoosh Range, the Goat Rocks, and Mount Adams. When you are ready, return to Paradise along the same trail.

Miles and Directions

0.0 Start hiking to the right (east) along the Skyline Trail in the northwestern corner of the parking lot.

0.4 Less than half a mile into your hike, come to a small trail to Myrtle Falls on your right (south) and the Golden Gate Trail junction on your left (north). You can take a peek at the falls, but come back to the Skyline Trail and continue east.

0.7 Reach the 4th Crossing Trail junction; stay to the left (east) along the Skyline Trail.

1.4 Stay to the left at the Lakes Trail junction.

1.8 When you spy a surreal rocky sofa in the middle of the trail, you know you have reached the Van Trump Monument junction and the Paradise Glacier Trail junction. Take the Paradise Glacier Trail to your right (northeast).

3.2 Arrive at Paradise Glacier. After exploring the snowfield, return the way you came.

6.4 Arrive back at the trailhead.

12 Snow Lake

Perfect for children, this medium-length day hike passes one lake and ends at a lake in a glacial cirque.

Start: Snow Lake trailhead.
Distance: 2.6-mile out-and-back.
Approximate hiking time: 1 to 2 hours.
Elevation gain: 700 feet.
Seasons: Mid-July through September.
Nearest towns: Ashford, Packwood.
Fees and permits: $10.00 vehicle or $5.00 individual entry fee (seven days); $30.00 annual entry fee. Wilderness Camping Permits free—reservations recommended ($20 fee).

Maps: USGS: Mount Rainier East; Trails Illustrated Mount Rainier National Park; Astronaut's Vista: Mount Rainier National Park, Washington; Earthwalk Press Hiking Map & Guide.
Trail contacts: Paradise Ranger Station, (360) 569-2211, ext. 2314.
Jackson Visitor Center—Paradise, (360) 569-6036.
Trail conditions: www.nps.gov/mora/trail/tr_cnd.htm; weather, www.nps.gov/mora/current/weather.htm.

Finding the trailhead: From the Stevens Canyon Entrance Station (see Getting There), drive 16.4 miles west along the winding Stevens Canyon Road. A small parking lot on the left (south) marks the trailhead to Snow Lake. From the Nisqually Entrance Station (see Getting There), travel nearly 16 miles east on Longmire-Paradise Road to the turnoff for the Ohanapecosh area. Turn right (southeast) onto Stevens Canyon Road and toward Ohanapecosh; follow this road for 3.0 miles

Snow Lake

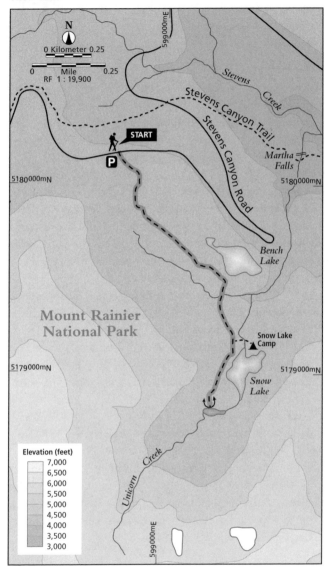

to the trailhead on your right (south). *DeLorme: Washington Atlas and Gazetteer:* Page 48 B3.

The Hike

Trees obscure the Snow Lake trailhead. When ready to hike, walk to the eastern corner of the parking lot to find the trail, heading south. The trail immediately begins to ascend rather steeply, but do not worry, it eventually levels off and descends, then crosses several ridges throughout the hike.

The trail leads 0.7 mile through silver subalpine forest to the junction with the path to Bench Lake on the left (east). The path down to the lake is steep, but the bank is worth the struggle, particularly if you fish. Though Bench lake is cursed by the evasive fish common throughout Mount Rainier, they do rise here, so you may want to pack that pole. Fishing permits are not required, and there are no limits on fish caught. Of course you may not fish for the endangered bull trout. Similar to brook trout, but identified by the lack of black markings on its dorsal fin, the bull trout is a federally listed species under the Environmental Protection Act. Follow the motto "No Black, Throw It Back" when fishing in Mount Rainier National Park, or face a guilty conscience and hefty fines.

Returning to the main trail, you only have 0.5 mile of hiking before you reach Snow Lake, named possibly because snow rings the lake nearly year-round. When you arrive at the mountain meadow, turn around. This area offers a beautiful view of Mount Rainier. And in the foreground, depending on the season, you can spy a variety of flowers, from glacier lilies to mountain bog gentian, beargrass, huckleberry bushes, and mountain ash.

The last 0.2 mile of trail slopes upward until you see the lovely tarn. In a glacial cirque, the peaks of the Tatoosh Range frame the lake, and glacial waters cascade down their flanks into the ice-cold aqua waters.

If you would like to camp here or see the marvelous view from the campsites, turn left (east) at the fork in the trail—a sign points the way. Descend for less than 0.2 mile until the trail crosses a stream out of Snow Lake. To cross this stream you must hop from log to log. Be careful—some of these logs are not quite as stable as they appear. As soon as you cross the stream, you reach Snow Lake Camp. The toilet is almost immediately to your left; the campsites are farther down (southeast) and along the lakeside. Site 1 sits on a small peninsula with a view of Unicorn Peak across the aqua waters. A jutting rock makes for a great place to jump in the freezing waters for a refreshing dunk or a painful swim. If you decide to stay at this idyllic spot, be sure to hang your food; black bears have been spotted here.

You can also follow the path to the right (southwest) at the fork before the lake. This path is 0.3 mile and ends in a small lake-access point. If you hike this trail, plan to spend some time at one of these places; they are lovely. When you're ready to return, just retrace your steps.

Miles and Directions

- **0.0** Start by walking to the eastern corner of the Snow Lake trailhead parking lot to find the trail, heading south.
- **0.7** A short trail heads to Bench Lake. If you want to see the lake or fish for a while, take the trail to the left (east). Otherwise, stay on the main trail to Snow Lake.
- **1.2** Reach the aqua glacial waters of Snow Lake. If you plan on visiting the camp, head left (east) for less than 0.2 mile.

1.3 After hopping carefully from log to log, arrive at Snow Lake Camp. Retrace your steps.

2.6 Arrive back at the trailhead.

13 **Stevens Creek**

A one-hour hike in the southern section of the park leads to two unnamed waterfalls along the same river.

Start: Box Canyon Picnic Area.
Distance: 1.4-mile out-and-back.
Approximate hiking time: 1 hour.
Elevation gain: Minimal.
Seasons: Late May through September.
Nearest towns: Ashford, Packwood.
Fees and permits: $10.00 vehicle or $5.00 individual entry fee (seven days); $30.00 annual entry fee. Wilderness Camping Permits free—reservations recommended ($20 fee).

Maps: USGS: Mount Rainier East; Trails Illustrated Mount Rainier National Park; Astronaut's Vista: Mount Rainier National Park, Washington; Earthwalk Press Hiking Map & Guide.
Trail contacts: Paradise Ranger Station, (360) 569-2211, ext. 2314.
Jackson Visitor Center—Paradise, (360) 569-6036.
Trail conditions: www.nps.gov/mora/trail/tr_cnd.htm; weather, www.nps.gov/mora/current/weather.htm

Finding the trailhead: From the Stevens Canyon Entrance Station (see Getting There), drive 10.8 miles west on Stevens Canyon Road to the Box Canyon Picnic Area on the left, about 0.3 mile beyond the Box Canyon wayside exhibit. From the Nisqually Entrance Station (see Getting There), travel nearly 16 miles east on Longmire-Paradise Road to the turnoff for the Ohanapecosh area. Turn right (southeast) onto Stevens Canyon Road and toward Ohanapecosh. Stay on this

Stevens Creek

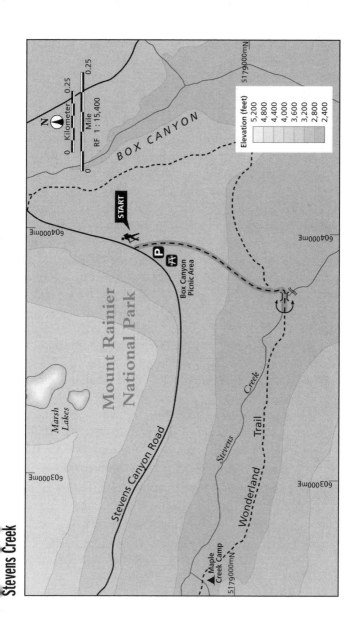

road for 8.6 miles until you reach the Box Canyon Picnic Area. The hike heads south from the picnic area. *DeLorme: Washington Atlas and Gazetteer:* Page 48 B3.

The Hike

This trail descends rather steeply through woods full of wildlife to reach two unnamed falls. Well marked and well maintained, the trail is easy to follow. The first point of interest comes after only 0.5 mile. A sign marks the river viewpoint to your right (west). Only a few paces more and you stand in a fenced clearing, admiring the first waterfall.

Return to the main trail and head right (south) to see the other nameless falls. Walk 0.1 mile beyond the river viewpoint, a total of 0.6 mile from the trailhead, to a junction with the famed Wonderland Trail. Stay to the right (southwest) for 0.1 mile more to reach the bridge over Stevens Creek.

This bridge marks an incredible meeting of stream and stone. Iceberg white water rushing from the glaciers above has rounded these boulders and shaped them into something out of a fairy tale.

When you have appreciated the falls to your content, turn around and follow the same path back to the picnic area. The returning trail is not long, but it is a rather steep ascent; do not be surprised if you are winded by the end.

Miles and Directions

0.0   Start heading south from the Box Canyon Picnic Area.

0.5   A sign points to a vista overlooking an unnamed waterfall. Check out the falls, then continue southwest on the main trail to the intersection with the Wonderland Trail.

0.6 At the junction with the Wonderland Trail, turn right (west) onto the Wonderland Trail.

0.7 Just after you get onto the Wonderland Trail, come to the Stevens Creek crossing. The bridge offers a great look at the multicolored boulders carved and smoothed by the waters of Stevens Creek. Enjoy the view before retracing your steps.

1.4 Arrive back at the trailhead.

14 Box Canyon

This very short loop crosses a bridge over a canyon carved by a powerful glacier.

Start: Box Canyon wayside exhibit.
Distance: 0.3-mile loop.
Approximate hiking time: 15 to 30 minutes.
Elevation gain: Minimal.
Seasons: May through September.
Nearest towns: Ashford, Packwood.
Fees and permits: $10.00 vehicle or $5.00 individual entry fee (seven days); $30.00 annual entry fee. Wilderness Camping Permits free—reservations recommended ($20 fee).

Maps: USGS: Mount Rainier East; Trails Illustrated Mount Rainier National Park; Astronaut's Vista: Mount Rainier National Park, Washington; Earthwalk Press Hiking Map & Guide.
Trail contacts: Paradise Ranger Station, (360) 569-2211, ext. 2314.
Jackson Visitor Center—Paradise, (360) 569-6036.
Trail conditions: www.nps.gov/mora/trail/tr_cnd.htm; weather, www.nps.gov/mora/current/weather.htm.

Finding the trailhead: From the Stevens Canyon Entrance Station (see Getting There), drive 10.5 miles west on Stevens Canyon Road

Box Canyon

Mount Rainier
National Park

Wonderland Trail

Stevens Canyon Road

START

Box Canyon
Exhibit

BOX CANYON

Muddy Fork Cowlitz River

Wonderland Trail

N

Kilometer
0   0.2

Mile
0   0.2

RF 1 : 8,800

Elevation (feet)
4,200
4,000
3,800
3,600
3,400
3,200
3,000
2,800
2,600

6045000mE

6040000mE

5180000mN

to the Box Canyon wayside exhibit. Parking is on the left (south). If you pass the Box Canyon Picnic Area, you have gone 0.3 mile too far west. From the Nisqually Entrance Station (see Getting There), travel nearly 16 miles east on Longmire-Paradise Road to the turnoff for the Ohanapecosh area. Turn right (southeast) onto Stevens Canyon Road and toward Ohanapecosh. Stay on this road for 9.0 miles until you reach the Box Canyon wayside exhibit, 0.3 mile past the Box Canyon Picnic Area. The paved trail begins across the street from the parking lot to the right (east) of the bridge. *DeLorme: Washington Atlas and Gazetteer:* Page 48 B3.

The Hike

This hike is great for those interested in glaciers. Many years ago a glacier gouged dirt and boulders out of the mountainside to create Box Canyon. The paved trail takes you past wildflowers and the thundering canyon itself. For the first half of this hike, the paved trail is wide, smooth, and wheelchair accessible. The entire hike is paved, but the second stretch is considerably rougher and would prove tumultuous travel for a wheelchair.

At the trailhead there is an informational sign about the hike. After reading it, head straight up the trail. The trail merging from the right (northeast) is the Wonderland Trail. Notice the bare rocks on the right side of the canyon, where a powerful glacier once wiped out the vegetation.

Less than 0.2 mile into your hike is a bridge over Muddy Fork. Take the time to look down and enjoy the unique canyon. After you cross the bridge, the trail is paved, but less maintained, all the way to where it rejoins Stevens Canyon Road. Either retrace your steps or walk along the road to loop back to your car.

Miles and Directions

0.0 Head north across the Stevens Canyon Roa from the Box Canyon Exhibit to the Box Canyon Trail, a short informative section of the Wonderland Trail.

0.1 At the bridge crossing the Muddy Fork of the the Cowlitz River, continue across the bridge to the other side of the loop.

0.2 The Wonderland Trail splits off on its route around Mount Rainier. Stay to the left (southeast) back to the Box Canyon Exibit.

0.3 Skirt the Stevens Canyon Road to reach the trailhead.

15 Silver Falls

This short, beautiful day hike takes you to spectacular Silver Falls.

Start: Silver Falls Loop trailhead/ Ohanapecosh Visitor Center.
Distance: 2.7-mile loop.
Approximate hiking time: 1 to 2 hours.
Elevation gain: Minimal.
Seasons: May through September.
Nearest town: Packwood.
Fees and permits: $10.00 vehicle or $5.00 individual entry fee (seven days); $30.00 annual entry fee. Wilderness Camping Permits free—reservations recommended ($20 fee).

Maps: USGS: Ohanapecosh Hot Springs and Chinook Pass; Trails Illustrated Mount Rainier National Park; Astronaut's Vista: Mount Rainier National Park, Washington; Earthwalk Press Hiking Map & Guide.
Trail contacts: Ohanapecosh Visitor Center, (360) 569-6046.
Trail conditions: www.nps.gov/ mora/trail/tr_cnd.htm; weather, www.nps.gov/mora/current/ weather.htm.

Finding the trailhead: From Packwood drive 7.0 miles northeast on U.S. Highway 12 to the junction with Highway 123. Turn left

Silver Falls

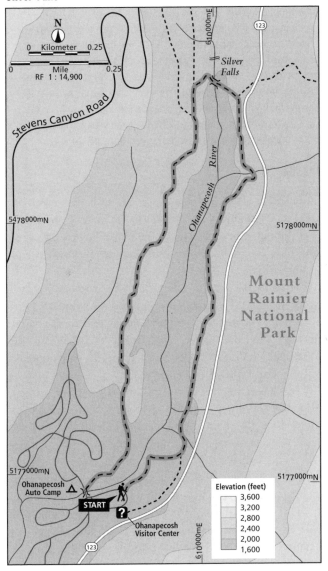

N

0   Kilometer   0.25

0   Mile   0.25
RF 1 : 14,900

Stevens Canyon Road

123

Silver Falls

Ohanapecosh River

5478000mN

610000mE

5178000mN

Mount Rainier National Park

5177000mN

5177000mN

Ohanapecosh Auto Camp

START

?

Ohanapecosh Visitor Center

610000mE

123

Elevation (feet)

3,600
3,200
2,800
2,400
2,000
1,600

(north) onto Highway 123 and continue for 3.0 miles to the turnoff for Ohanapecosh Campground, just 1.8 miles south of the Stevens Canyon Entrance Station (see Getting There). Turn left (west) and immediately right again at the fork in the road toward the campground. Continue on this road as it winds past the visitor center. Go right (north) toward the day parking area. Loop around to enter the parking lot from the other (east) side. On the way you will see the Silver Falls trailhead to your left (north). Park and walk to the trailhead. *DeLorme: Washington Atlas and Gazetteer:* Page 48 B4, C4.

The Hike

Silver Falls opens early in the year due to its low elevation, and visitors can enjoy the falls as early as May. The trail wanders through a beautiful forest. Traffic can be very heavy on this trail, since the trailhead is located at Ohanapecosh Campground.

The first 0.1 mile of this hike is also part of an educational self-guided loop trail that explains the Mount Rainier ecosystem. The numbered posts along the trail correspond to text in an interpretive pamphlet available in the Ohanapecosh Visitor Center. Stay left (north) when the Hot Springs Trail forks off to the right.

The beginning of the trail runs through a thermal area. You will see hot springs and interpretive signs telling you more about the thermal features. The ground is fragile and easily damaged here, making it especially important that you stay on the trail. Walking off the trail in this area is illegal, and park officials may cite violators. Remember that water originating from hot springs is unsafe for human consumption.

The trail gains a bit of elevation in the beginning. You will cross two bridges before you reach the bridge over Laughingwater Creek. The first bridge is more than 0.1 mile into your hike; the second bridge is a little less than 0.8 mile. Both of these bridges cross streams that empty into the Ohanapecosh River, which is to your left (west). At 0.9 mile you reach Laughingwater Creek, aptly named as the water bounces and frolics over the rocks. Cross Laughingwater Creek and walk 0.1 mile to the Laughingwater Trail junction. Stay to the left and on the Silver Falls Loop.

Silver Falls is 0.2 mile from the Laughingwater Trail junction, 1.2 miles into your hike. An overlook, 0.1 mile from where you first see the falls, faces the shining waters of Silver Falls. Take your time and enjoy the marvelous view until you are ready to move on. We must emphasize that the rocks at Silver Falls are moss covered and slippery. People have lost their lives as a result of disregarding the warning signs posted by the falls. Please stay behind the guardrails.

The second half of the loop is not as eventful as the first half, but the trail winds through a pleasant mixture of western hemlock, Douglas fir, and western red cedar. The trail exits at a different location from where it began; simply walk over the bridge and head back to the day parking lot.

Miles and Directions

0.0 Start at the trailhead near the Ohanapecosh Visitor Center.

0.1 Hot Springs Trail forks to the right; stay to the left (north) on the Silver Falls Trail.

1.0 At the Laughingwater Trail junction, stay to the left (north). Again, head toward Silver Falls.

1.2 Enjoy Silver Falls, but stay behind the barricades.

1.4 Just 0.2 mile beyond Silver Falls and the Silver Falls overlook, reach the Eastside Trail. Take a sharp left (south), heading back toward the Ohanapecosh Visitor Center and Campground.

1.5 Stay to the left (south) at the Cowlitz Divide Trail junction.

2.7 The end of the loop drops you off at the Ohanapecosh Campground, just north of the trailhead.

16 Grove of the Patriarchs

This short interpretive hike takes you through magnificent old-growth forest.

Start: Grove of the Patriarchs parking lot.
Distance: 1.1-mile lollipop.
Approximate hiking time: 1 hour.
Elevation gain: Minimal.
Seasons: May through September.
Nearest town: Packwood.
Fees and permits: $10.00 vehicle or $5.00 individual entry fee (seven days); $30.00 annual entry fee. Wilderness Camping Permits free—reservations recommended ($20 fee).

Maps: USGS: Chinook Pass; Trails Illustrated Mount Rainier National Park; Astronaut's Vista: Mount Rainier National Park, Washington; Earthwalk Press Hiking Map & Guide.
Trail contacts: Ohanapecosh Visitor Center, (360) 569-6046.
Trail conditions: www.nps.gov/ mora/trail/tr_cnd.htm; weather, www.nps.gov/mora/current/ weather.htm.

Finding the trailhead: From Stevens Canyon Entrance Station (see Getting There), go west 0.2 mile on Stevens Canyon Road to a parking lot on your right (north), marked by a sign that reads GROVE OF THE PATRIARCHS. The trailhead is to the right (west) of the restrooms. *DeLorme: Washington Atlas and Gazetteer:* Page 48 B4.

The Hike

The trail is very well maintained but often muddy, due to its low elevation and proximity to the Ohanapecosh River. Wear

Grove of the Patriarchs

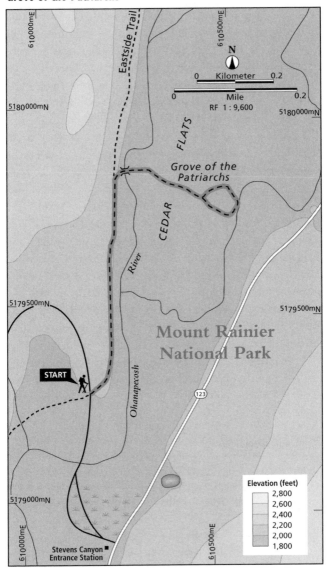

your hiking boots, and remember to step through the mud instead of around it to avoid widening the trails. Interpretive signs line the trail, helping you discern differences between the western hemlock, Douglas fir, and western red cedar. This is a great trail to take if you are interested in learning more about the life cycles and species of old-growth forests.

The Ohanapecosh River flows on your right for the first 0.3 mile as the trail meanders through old-growth forest. The waters flow abnormally clearly for a glacial river; the inactivity of the Ohanapecosh Glacier reduces the amount of suspended glacial flour.

The trail forks 0.3 mile into the hike. The Eastside Trail continues heading north; the Grove of the Patriarchs Trail veers off to the right (southeast) toward a steel suspension bridge over the Ohanapecosh River. The bridge links to an island rich with old-growth forest. Some of the trees towering over the forest floor are more than 1,000 years old.

Around 0.1 mile past the Grove of the Patriarchs junction, the trail splits to form a loop. Go left (northeast) around the loop. Make sure to check out the humbling height of the red cedar about halfway through the loop. Continue along the loop until you are back to the stem of the lollipop. The return trip gives you a chance to apply your newfound tree identification skills.

Miles and Directions

0.0 Follow the signs to the Grove of the Patrairchs and the Eastside Trail, heading east on the right of the restrooms. The trail quickly turns north to parallel the crystal clear Ohanapecosh River.

0.3 The Grove of the Patriarachs Trail splinters off the Eastside Trail to cross the Ohanapecosh River.

0.4 The stem of the lollipop trail splits in two; we recommend going left around this loop section.

1.1 Return the way you came to reach parking lot.

1 7 Naches Peak

A popular loop in summer, Naches Peak Trail offers small mountain lakes, subalpine forest, good views of Mount Rainier, and a worthwhile side trip to Dewey Lake.

Start: Naches Peak trailhead.
Distance: 5.0-mile loop.
Approximate hiking time: 2 hours.
Elevation gain: Minimal.
Seasons: Late July through September.
Nearest town: Greenwater.
Fees and permits: Possible fee for use of the national forest (Dewey Lake).
Maps: USGS: Chinook Pass; Trails Illustrated Mount Rainier National Park; Astronaut's Vista: Mount Rainier National Park, Washington; Earthwalk Press Hiking Map & Guide.
Trail contacts: White River Wilderness Information Center, (360) 569-6030.
Trail conditions: www.nps.gov/mora/trail/tr_cnd.htm; weather, www.nps.gov/mora/current/weather.htm.

Finding the trailhead: From the junction of Highways 410 and 123 on the eastern edge of the park, drive east on Highway 410 to Chinook Pass. Continue east, out of the park, and park in the Tipsoo Lake parking lot on the right (south) side of the road just west of Chinook Pass. Walk west along the highway for less than 0.5 mile to the large park entrance sign above the road. The top of the sign doubles as a bridge; the trailhead sign is on the north side of the bridge. *DeLorme: Washington Atlas and Gazetteer:* Page 48 A4.

Naches Peak

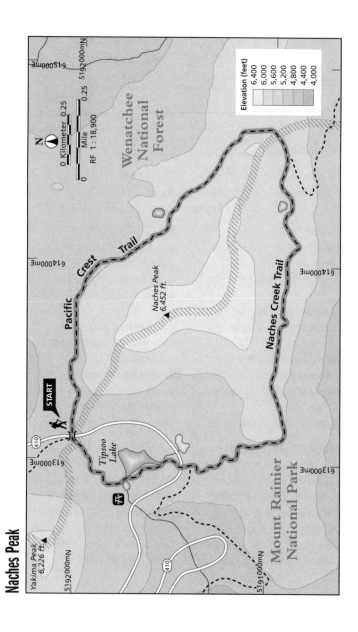

Elevation (feet)
6,400
6,000
5,600
5,200
4,800
4,400
4,000

N

0 Kilometer 0.25
0 Mile 0.25
RF 1 : 18,900

Pacific Crest Trail

Wenatchee National Forest

Naches Peak 6,452 ft.

Naches Creek Trail

Mount Rainier National Park

START

410

Tipsoo Lake

Yakima Peak 6,226 ft.

410

6150000mE
5192000mN
6144000mE
6143000mE
6140000mE
5191000mN
5192000mN

The Hike

For good reason, the loop around Naches Peak is a very popular hike. The first 2.0 miles of trail are outside the park and along the Pacific Crest Trail. Because this part of the Naches Peak loop is pet-friendly, you may see many hikers with leashed dogs and the occasional horseback rider. If you have a pet you would like to walk, however, you cannot complete the loop. Because pets are not allowed on the section of trail inside park boundaries, you must turn around at the park entrance signs where the Naches Peak Trail intersects the Pacific Crest Trail.

From the Naches Peak trailhead, cross the bridge to the southeast side of Highway 410. The trail ascends steadily, passing a few small subalpine lakes. Trails lead to the lakes, but they are not maintained, and trekking through such fragile meadow is discouraged. Stay on the trail.

The trail reaches its highest point just before entering the park and curves eastward. Soon, 2.2 miles into the hike, the Pacific Crest Trail branches left (south) toward Dewey Lake; the Naches Peak Loop continues straight ahead (west).

Continuing along the Naches Peak Trail, you round the bend to catch a great view of Mount Rainier. In fact, this part of the hike boasts some of the most spectacular views of the entire eastern slope. If you have a map, you can try to identify Little Tahoma, the Cowlitz Chimneys, Governors Ridge, and Seymour Peak to the west.

The trail wraps to the right, around Naches Peak. Wildflowers blanket the meadows in midsummer; huckleberries do the same in late summer. The trail also passes a small mountain lake on this side of the peak. As the trail turns north, you can see Tipsoo Lake, with its parking lot and picnic tables.

To reach the picnic area, 4.6 miles into the hike, you must cross Highway 410. The continuing trail is visible across the road. A maintained trail loops around Tipsoo Lake, if you are up for a casual stroll.

The steepest incline on the hike is left for the end. The trail passes just north of the picnic area, switches back a few times, then sets you back at the trailhead. Walk east along Highway 410 to return to your car.

Miles and Directions

0.0   Start heading east on the Pacific Crest Trail/Naches Peak Trail on the path that goes over the MOUNT RAINIER NATIONAL PARK ENTRANCE sign that straddles Highway 410 at the park boundary.

2.2   Almost halfway through the loop, the Pacific Crest Trail spurs off to the left (south) and heads toward Dewey Lake, a side trip option for this hike.

4.6   Reach Highway 410; the trail continues on the other side.

4.7   Arrive at the banks of Tipsoo Lake just after crossing the road.

5.0   After skirting the lake and climbing in forest, you have come full circle back to Highway 410.

18 Dege Peak

A short climb to the top of Dege Peak affords views of Mount Rainier, the North Cascades, Mount Adams, Mount Baker, and Sunrise Lake.

Start: Sunrise Point.
Distance: 2.8-mile out-and-back.
Approximate hiking time: 1 to 2 hours.
Elevation gain: 928 feet.
Seasons: Mid-July through September.
Nearest town: Greenwater.
Fees and permits: $10.00 vehicle or $5.00 individual entry fee (seven days); $30.00 annual entry fee.
Maps: USGS: White River Park;
Trails Illustrated Mount Rainier National Park; Astronaut's Vista: Mount Rainier National Park, Washington; Earthwalk Press Hiking Map & Guide.
Trail contacts: White River Wilderness Information Center, (360) 569-6030.
Trail conditions: www.nps.gov/mora/trail/tr_cnd.htm; weather, www.nps.gov/mora/current/weather.htm.

Finding the trailhead: From the White River Ranger Station (see Getting There), continue 11.0 miles on White River Road to well-marked Sunrise Point. *DeLorme: Washington Atlas and Gazetteer:* Page 48 A4.

Special considerations: There is a sizable parking lot at Sunrise Point, but it is often busy. If the parking lot is full, parking along the road is not an option. Instead, consider climbing Dege Peak from the west side. (See Option.)

The Hike

Although this hike is only 2.8 miles long, you climb uphill for the entire 1.4-mile trip to Dege Peak. Make sure to

Dege Peak

N

Kilometer 0.25 0 0.25

Mile 0.25 0 0.25

RF 1 : 15,300

Mount Rainier National Park

Sunrise Lake

START

Sunrise Point

P

White River Road

Sourdough Ridge Trail

White River Road

Dege Peak Trail

Dege Peak 7,008 ft.

607000mE

607000mE

606000mE

606000mE

5197000mN

Elevation (feet)
7,200
6,800
6,400
6,000
5,600
5,200
4,800
4,400

bring plenty of water, and pace yourself throughout the climb. From the top of Dege Peak, jaw-dropping scenery surrounds you in every direction.

The Sourdough Ridge Trail begins from the west end of the parking lot; head west. Subalpine wildflowers, such as lupine and magenta paintbrush, often line the trail in midsummer, and trees provide much-needed shade on a hot day. Marcus Peak rises on the right (north), and when you have gained enough elevation, Mount Rainier comes into view to the west.

After hiking 1.1 miles, you come to the junction with the Dege Peak Trail. Turn right (northeast) on this trail. It is only 0.3 mile to the summit from this point, but the trail follows steep switchbacks all the way to the top. At the top of Dege Peak you have entered the alpine zone. The peak consists of rock; little vegetation grows on the rocky surface. You can see two dormant volcanoes, Mount Baker and Mount Adams, and enjoy an impressive view of majestic Mount Rainier.

When you decide to head back, it is all downhill! Relish the view of Clover and Sunrise Lakes as you descend the peak. Sunrise Lake is closest to Sunrise Point, where you began your hike; Clover Lake is farther north, near Marcus Peak.

Miles and Directions

- **0.0** Start heading west on the Sourdough Ridge Trail from the west end of the Sunrise Point parking lot.
- **1.1** At the junction with the Dege Peak Trail, turn right (north) and begin the steep climb to Dege Peak.

1.4 Reach Dege Peak summit. Enjoy the view and then begin your descent.

2.8 Arrive back at the trailhead.

Option: If the parking lot is full, or if you want to start from the Sunrise Complex, park in the Sunrise parking lot, 2.6 miles west from Sunrise Point on White River Road. There is a huge parking lot there, but on a sunny weekend it, too, might be full. If it is, you might have to choose an alternative hike.

From the Sunrise Complex, head up the paved path to the right of the restrooms leading to the Sourdough Ridge Nature Trail. Turn right (northeast) up the nature trail and stay on it for a little over 0.3 mile to the junction with the Sourdough Ridge Trail. Turn right (east) onto the Sourdough Ridge Trail and head east toward Dege Peak, which is 1.5 miles away. This option has a total out-and-back distance of 3.8 miles.

19 Sourdough Ridge Nature Trail

This is a one-hour self-guiding informative stroll along Sourdough Ridge.

Start: Sunrise Complex.
Distance: 1.5-mile lollipop.
Approximate hiking time: 1 hour.
Elevation gain: Minimal.
Seasons: Mid-July through September.
Nearest town: Greenwater.
Fees and permits: $10.00 vehicle or $5.00 individual entry fee (seven days); $30.00 annual entry fee.

Maps: USGS: Sunrise; Trails Illustrated Mount Rainier National Park; Astronaut's Vista: Mount Rainier National Park, Washington; Earthwalk Press Hiking Map & Guide.
Trail contacts: White River Wilderness Information Center, (360) 569-6030.
Trail conditions: www.nps.gov/mora/trail/tr_cnd.htm; weather, www.nps.gov/mora/current/weather.htm.

Finding the trailhead: From the White River Entrance Station (see Getting There), drive 13.8 miles west on the White River Road to the Sunrise Complex parking lot. Park and walk to the trailhead on the northwestern end of the lot, to the right of the restrooms. *DeLorme: Washington Atlas and Gazetteer:* Page 48 A3.

The Hike

To begin this hike, go to the northwestern part of the parking lot. Follow the wide trail running north beyond the restrooms. About 0.1 mile into the hike, a map and display on the right (east) delineate some of the trails in the Sunrise area, including elevation charts and short descriptions. Left

Sourdough Ridge Nature Trail

Elevation (feet)
7,200
6,900
6,600
6,300
6,000
5,700
5,400

N

Kilometer
0   0.25   0.25

Mile
0   RF 1:9,700

SOURDOUGH MOUNTAINS

Sourdough Ridge Nature Trail

Sourdough Ridge Nature Trail

Sourdough Ridge Nature Trail

Sourdough Ridge Nature Trail

Sourdough Ridge Trail

Mount Rainier National Park

START

Sunrise Ranger Station

P

Sunrise Visitor Center

?

YAKIMA PARK

603000mE

603500mE

5197000mN

5196500mN

(north) of the map, a small box holds the accompanying pamphlet to Sourdough Ridge Nature Trail, entitled *sourdough ridge: subalpine meadow ecology*. If you plan to keep this pamphlet, put 50 cents in the fee box. Otherwise, return the pamphlet upon completion of the hike.

Continue north on this trail until it forks. Follow the sign pointing right (east). For Stations 1 through 7, you walk along the south slope of Sourdough Ridge. You have a fantastic view of the grandeur of Mount Rainier, while the stations inform you about the small but crucial parts of the ecosystem.

After Station 7, the path forks. Take the left (west) fork. From Stations 8 to 13, you walk along the top of Sourdough Ridge with views off both sides of the ridge. On a clear day you can see Mount Baker, Mount Adams, and Glacier Peak.

After Station 13 turn left (south). The Sunrise Complex comes into sight, as the lollipop reaches its end. As the pamphlet says, "We hope this walk has given you a look behind the scenery, into the ever changing environmental forces that influence this subalpine community."

20 Silver Forest

Enjoy an easy one-hour walk to informative viewpoints along a flowery subalpine meadow.

Start: Sunrise Complex.
Distance: 2.0-mile out-and-back.
Approximate hiking time: 1 hour.
Elevation gain: Minimal.
Seasons: Mid-July through September.
Nearest town: Greenwater.
Fees and permits: $10.00 vehicle or $5.00 individual entry fee (seven days); $30.00 annual entry fee.

Maps: USGS: Sunrise and White River Park; Trails Illustrated Mount Rainier National Park; Astronaut's Vista: Mount Rainier National Park, Washington; Earthwalk Press Hiking Map & Guide.
Trail contacts: White River Wilderness Information Center, (360) 569-6030.
Trail conditions: www.nps.gov/mora/trail/tr_cnd.htm; weather, www.nps.gov/mora/current/weather.htm.

Finding the trailhead: From the White River Entrance Station (see Getting There), drive 13.8 miles west on White River Road to the Sunrise Complex parking lot. Park in one of the many spaces provided. The trailhead is south of the parking lot. *DeLorme: Washington Atlas and Gazetteer:* Page 48 A3.

The Hike

The Silver Forest Trail involves two parts. First, a short descent leads to two informative exhibits with great views of Mount Rainier. Then the trail continues east through subalpine forest and meadow.

Silver Forest

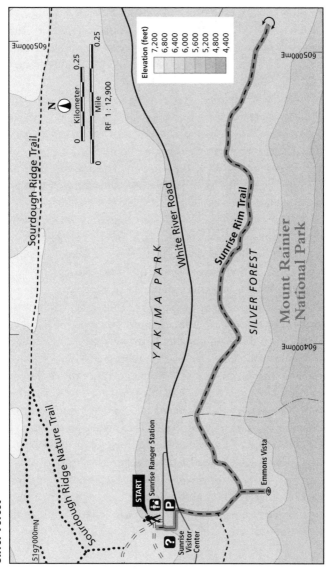

Silver Forest

START

Sourdough Ridge Nature Trail

Sourdough Ridge Trail

Sunrise Ranger Station

Sunrise Visitor Center

YAKIMA PARK

White River Road

Sunrise Rim Trail

SILVER FOREST

Emmons Vista

Mount Rainier
National Park

N

Kilometer 0.25

0   0.25 Mile

RF 1 : 12,900

Elevation (feet)
7,200
6,800
6,400
6,000
5,600
5,200
4,800
4,400

5197000mN

605000mE

604000mE

605000mE

To find the trailhead, park in the Sunrise parking lot. From the south side of the lot, directly across from the ranger station and cafeteria, a trail heads south and a dirt road heads west. As the sign directs, follow the southbound trail, the Emmons Vista Nature Trail.

In only 0.1 mile you reach the junction with the Sunrise Rim Trail. Stay to the left (south). The path curves east, and a sign points south to the first Emmons Vista exhibit. Walk down to the viewpoint and admire the tree-framed view of the Emmons and Winthrop Glaciers. The exhibit explains the various features of a glaciated mountain and how they were formed.

Return to the main trail and continue east. You soon come upon the second exhibit, again immediately south of the trail. This vista point has a nice, sheltered seating area and two more informative signs. The first, SNOW SHADOW, includes climatic information about the winds and snow of Paradise. The other, ROCKS RIDING ON AIR, gives a historical account of the Little Tahoma Peak rockslide of 1963.

Back on the main trail, head east once again. In less than 0.1 mile, you come to a sign indicating that you have reached the Silver Forest portion of the trail. A fire of unknown origins incinerated this area long ago. Today the only remnants of the old forest are "silver sentinels," long-dead but standing trees. In the fire's wake, subalpine trees and wildflowers have grown, making this forest particularly intriguing. Small, gnarled trees are dispersed throughout this meadow, along with blankets of violet flowers in midsummer. Walk along this trail for 0.8 mile before reaching a sign that indicates the end of the maintained trail, 1.0 mile from the trailhead. The trail continues for quite some distance beyond this sign, so venture farther if you want an extended hike. Otherwise, turn around and walk back to the Sunrise Complex.

Miles and Directions

0.0   Start heading south on the trail across the parking lot from the snack bar and gift shop.

0.1   In just a short while, reach the juncture of the Emmons Vista and Sunrise Rim Trails. Stay to the left (east) toward the Emmons Vista exhibits.

0.2   There are two Emmons Vista exhibits, one with information on glaciation and one on climatic conditions. Both have viewpoints.

1.0   The trail heads through silver forest and peters out. Retrace your steps.

2.0   Arrive back at the trailhead.

21 Emmons Moraine

A short hike up to the Emmons Moraine provides an excellent view of the Emmons Glacier, the largest glacier in the contiguous United States.

Start: Glacier Basin trailhead.
Distance: 2.8-mile out-and-back.
Approximate hiking time: 1 to 2 hours.
Elevation gain: 960 feet.
Seasons: Early July through September.
Nearest town: Greenwater.
Fees and permits: $10.00 vehicle or $5.00 individual entry fee (seven days); $30.00 annual entry fee.

Maps: USGS: Sunrise; Trails Illustrated Mount Rainier National Park; Astronaut's Vista: Mount Rainier National Park, Washington; Earthwalk Press Hiking Map & Guide.
Trail contacts: White River Wilderness Information Center, (360) 569–6030.
Trail conditions: www.nps.gov/mora/trail/tr_cnd.htm; weather, www.nps.gov/mora/current/weather.htm.

Finding the trailhead: From the White River Entrance Station (see Getting There), drive 4.0 miles west on White River Road to the White River Campground turnoff. Turn left (northwest) toward the campground, and drive another mile to the parking area on the left. A sign indicates that the parking lot is for backpackers and climbers. Park here and walk to the Glacier Basin trailhead on the west side of Loop D, one of the many loops that make up White River Campground. *DeLorme: Washington Atlas and Gazetteer:* Page 48 A3.

The Hike

This short, gradual uphill hike is great for children. Hike along the Emmons Moraine for a close-up view of the

Emmons Moraine

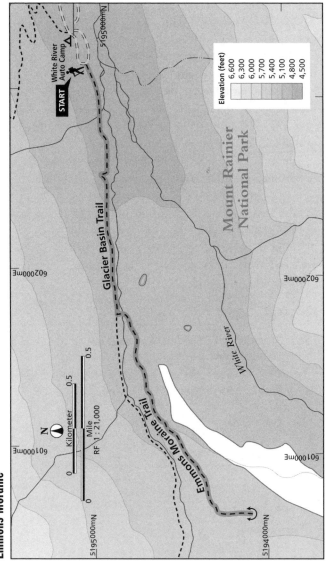

Emmons Glacier. At one time the Emmons Glacier filled the whole valley here, carving an amazingly flat and expansive section out of the earth.

Head west along the Glacier Basin Trail. Very near the beginning of the trail, you come to an informational billboard about this hike and other hikes in the immediate area. From here hike 0.9 mile through tranquil forest to the junction with the Emmons Moraine Trail. At the junction go left (southwest), up the Emmons Moraine Trail.

Travel slightly uphill for another 0.5 mile to the end of the maintained trail. Your feet sink into the sandy trail formed from silt deposits by the Emmons Glacier. On a hot day the sand soaks up the sun, adding to the scorching heat, and the small trees along the Emmons Moraine provide little or no shade. Be sure to bring sunscreen. When you have marveled at the Emmons Glacier long enough, head back the same way you came.

Miles and Directions

0.0 Start heading west on the Glacier Basin Trail from Loop D of the White River Campground.

0.9 Emmons Moraine Trail separates from the Glacier Basin Trail toward the left (southwest); take the Emmons Moraine spur trail.

1.4 Emmons Moraine Trail ends with a view of the glacial wake. Enjoy the view before heading back the way you came.

2.8 Arrive back at the trailhead.

22 Mount Fremont Lookout

This hike makes a short ascent to a fire lookout on Mount Fremont that towers over the north side of the park. The lookout affords great views of Mount Rainier, Skyscraper Mountain, Grand Park, and Sourdough Ridge.

Start: Sunrise Complex.
Distance: 5.4-mile out-and-back.
Approximate hiking time: 2 to 4 hours.
Elevation gain: 781 feet.
Seasons: Early July through September.
Nearest town: Greenwater.
Fees and permits: $10.00 vehicle or $5.00 individual entry fee (seven days); $30.00 annual entry fee.

Maps: USGS: Sunrise; Trails Illustrated Mount Rainier National Park; Astronaut's Vista: Mount Rainier National Park, Washington; Earthwalk Press Hiking Map & Guide.
Trail contacts: White River Wilderness Information Center, (360) 569–6030.
Trail conditions: www.nps.gov/mora/trail/tr_cnd.htm; weather, www.nps.gov/mora/current/weather.htm.

Finding the trailhead: From the White River Entrance Station (see Getting There), drive 13.8 miles west on the White River Road to the Sunrise Complex parking lot. Park and walk to the trailhead on the northwestern end of the lot, to the right of the restrooms. *DeLorme: Washington Atlas and Gazetteer:* Page 48 A3.

The Hike

Walk up the paved path to the right (east) of the restrooms until you see a dirt trail on your right (north). Get on that trail and travel north until you come to the junction with

Mount Fremont Lookout

Mount Fremont Lookout

Mount Fremont
7,181 ft.

Forest Lake
5,600 ft.

Forest Lake Camp

McNeeley Peak
6,786 ft.

Mount Rainier National Park

HUCKLEBERRY BASIN

Frozen Lake

Mount Fremont Trail

Sourdough Ridge Trail

Sourdough Ridge Nature Trail

YAKIMA PARK

START

Sunrise Ranger Station

White River Road

N

RF 1:29,000

Kilometer 0.5

Mile 0.5

Elevation (feet)
7,600
7,200
6,800
6,400
6,000
5,600
5,200

604000mE
5198000mN
602000mE
601000mE
600000mE
5198000mN

the Sourdough Ridge Nature Trail. Turn left (northwest) onto the nature trail and walk 0.2 mile to the Sourdough Ridge Trail. Turn left (west) onto the Sourdough Ridge Trail.

While you are walking along this trail, you can see the North Cascades to your right. Mount Rainier also looms magnificent from Sourdough Ridge. After 0.3 mile you pass the Huckleberry Creek Trail on your right, heading northwest. Keep going west (left) another 0.8 mile to a five-way junction, immediately after Frozen Lake and 1.4 miles from the trailhead. At this junction the Mount Fremont Trail is the first trail on your right; follow it, heading north. The trail runs above timberline for the remainder of the hike. Fat marmots inhabit the green meadows along the trail. Keep in mind that it is illegal to feed animals and detrimental to their natural survival skills.

Soon the trail threads along the rocky side of Mount Fremont. Watch your step—the ledge drops straight off the ridge! Low-growing subalpine wildflowers line the trail in late July. Walk along the ridge until you reach the lookout, 2.7 miles from the Sunrise Complex. From the lookout you can see all the way to the north end of the park, where clearcuts begin to shave indiscriminate splotches in the forest. Skyscraper Mountain is to your left, just beyond the deep green and flower fields of Berkeley Park. North of Berkeley Park you can easily identify Grand Park, a massive plateau dappled with ghost trees. Mount Rainier towers above it all. Take the time to get out your map and identify the landmarks around you.

Miles and Directions

0.0 Start from the Sunrise parking lot, and follow the paved path to the right (east) of the restrooms, heading north. Don't let the road heading off to the left (west) tempt you; stay on the main trail, heading north past the informative display.

0.1 The Sourdough Ridge Nature Trail forks; stay to the left (northwest) toward Frozen Lake and Mount Fremont.

0.3 Reach the top of Sourdough Ridge and the junction with the Sourdough Ridge Nature Trail. Take a left (west) onto the trail.

0.6 Bypass the steep Huckleberry Creek Trail on your right (north).

1.4 Just beyond Frozen Lake, come to the Mount Fremont Trail junction. Follow the trail to the right (north).

2.7 Just over a mile of uphill along a rocky mountain slope and you can see Mount Fremont Lookout. Enjoy the view, and then retrace your steps.

5.4 Arrive back at the trailhead.

23 Forest Lake

A short descent over rocky alpine terrain travels through subalpine meadows to a quaint mountain lake.

Start: Sunrise Complex.
Distance: 5.0-mile out-and-back.
Approximate hiking time: 2 to 3 hours.
Elevation gain: 1,200 feet.
Seasons: Mid-July through September.
Nearest town: Greenwater.
Fees and permits: $10.00 vehicle or $5.00 individual entry fee (seven days); $30.00 annual entry fee. Wilderness Camping Permits free—reservations recommended ($20 fee).

Maps: USGS: Sunrise; Trails Illustrated Mount Rainier National Park; Astronaut's Vista: Mount Rainier National Park, Washington; Earthwalk Press Hiking Map & Guide.
Trail contacts: White River Wilderness Information Center, (360) 569-6030.
Trail conditions: www.nps.gov/ mora/trail/tr_cnd.htm; weather, www.nps.gov/mora/current/ weather.htm.

Finding the trailhead: From the White River Entrance Station (see Getting There), drive 13.8 miles west on White River Road to the Sunrise Complex parking lot. Park and walk to the trailhead on the north end of the lot, to the right of the restrooms. *DeLorme: Washington Atlas and Gazetteer:* Page 48 A4.

The Hike

If you want to escape the crowd at Sunrise and experience a variety of different ecosystems, this is the hike for you. From the tundra on the north side of Sourdough Ridge to the deciduous forest that surrounds Forest Lake, you will have a taste of everything.

Forest Lake

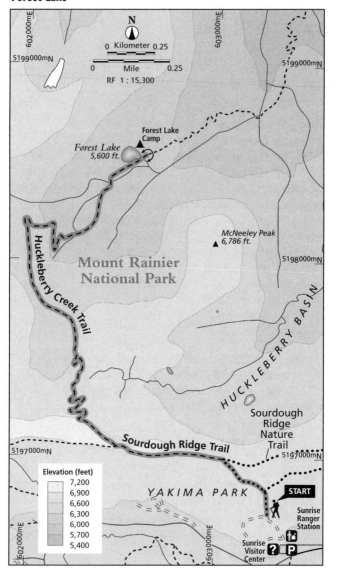

N

Kilometer	0.25
0	
0	Mile	0.25

RF 1 : 15,300

602000mE

5199000mN

603000mE

5199000mN

Forest Lake
Camp

Forest Lake
5,600 ft.

Huckleberry Creek Trail

Mount Rainier
National Park

McNeeley Peak
6,786 ft.

5198000mN

HUCKLEBERRY BASIN

Sourdough
Ridge
Nature
Trail

Sourdough Ridge Trail

5197000mN

5197000mN

Elevation (feet)

	7,200
	6,900
	6,600
	6,300
	6,000
	5,700
	5,400

YAKIMA PARK

START

Sunrise
Ranger
Station

602000mE

603000mE

Sunrise
Visitor
Center

Walk up the paved path to the right (east) of the restrooms until the trail forks. Take the dirt trail on your right (north). Walk up that trail until you come to the junction with the Sourdough Ridge Nature Trail. Turn left (northwest) onto the nature trail and walk 0.2 mile to the Sourdough Ridge Trail. Turn left (west) onto the Sourdough Ridge Trail.

While you are walking along this trail, you can see the Cascades to the north, and Mount Rainier looks magnificent from here. Soon the Huckleberry Creek Trail splits right. Take the Huckleberry Creek Trail, 0.6 mile into your hike. The trail briefly ascends and then begins a long descent to Forest Lake. The first part of the trail is in the alpine zone and relatively rocky. There are low-growing wildflowers, such as red mountain heather, all around. Patches of snow might linger on the trail until August, but the trail is usually easy to follow.

Keep your eyes open for wildlife on both Mount Fremont, to your left, and McNeeley Peak, to your right. Visible from Sourdough Ridge, the lush Huckleberry Basin lies between the two peaks.

Soon the trail heads into the trees and wanders through forest and meadows, overflowing with wildflowers in late July, all the way to Forest Lake. Forest Lake is small but charming. There is a great place right next to the campsite to take a break and enjoy the lake.

Miles and Directions

0.0 Start from the Sunrise parking lot; follow the paved path to the right (east) of the restrooms heading north. Don't let the road heading off to the left (west) tempt you; stay on the main trail, heading north past the informative display.

0.1	The Sourdough Ridge Nature Trail forks; stay to the left (northwest) toward Frozen Lake and Mount Fremont.
0.3	Reach the top of Sourdough Ridge and the junction with the Sourdough Ridge Nature Trail. Take a left (west) onto the trail.
0.6	Turn right (north) onto the Huckleberry Creek Trail, heading sharply down the hillside.
2.5	At Forest Lake and the Forest Lake Camp, you have reached your destination. Enjoy! Then head back the way you came.
5.0	Arrive back at the trailhead.

24 Sunrise Rim

This loop travels past Shadow Lake, over the first hump of Burroughs Mountain, to an overlook of the Emmons Glacier.

Start: Sunrise Complex.
Distance: 4.9-mile loop.
Approximate hiking time: 2 hours.
Elevation gain: 840 feet.
Seasons: August through September.
Nearest town: Greenwater.
Fees and permits: $10.00 vehicle or $5.00 individual entry fee (seven days); $30.00 annual entry fee. Wilderness Camping Permits free-reservations recommended ($20 fee).

Maps: USGS: Sunrise and White River Park, Mount Rainier East and Ohanapecosh Hot Springs; Trails Illustrated Mount Rainier National Park; Astronaut's Vista: Mount Rainier National Park, Washington; Earthwalk Press Hiking Map & Guide.
Trail contacts: White River Wilderness Information Center, (360) 569–6030.
Trail conditions: www.nps.gov/mora/trail/tr_cnd.htm; weather, www.nps.gov/mora/current/weather.htm.

Sunrise Rim

Sourdough Ridge Trail
Sourdough Ridge Nature Trail
Huckleberry Creek Trail
Mount Fremont Trail
Frozen Lake
Mount Rainier National Park
Wonderland Trail
Burroughs Mountain Trail
Sourdough Ridge Trail
YAKIMA PARK
Sunrise Visitor Center
START
Emmons Vista
Sunrise Rim Trail
Sunrise Rim Trail
Shadow Lake
Sunrise Camp
Burroughs Mountain Trail

Elevation (feet)
7,500
7,000
6,500
6,000
5,500
5,000
4,500

N

0 Kilometer 0.25

0 Mile 0.25

RF 1 : 20,933

603000mE
601000mE
5197000mN
5196000mN

Finding the trailhead: From the White River Entrance Station (see Getting There), drive 13.8 miles west on White River Road to the Sunrise Complex parking lot. Park and walk to the trailhead on the north end of the lot, to the right of the restrooms. *DeLorme: Washington Atlas and Gazetteer:* Page 48 A4.

The Hike

Great for kids and adults alike, this hike explores the scenic area around the Sunrise Complex. You walk along Sourdough Ridge, climb to the first hump of Burroughs Mountain, and look over the Emmons Glacier. It is rare to cover such a wide range of landscapes and see such incredible views in such a short hike.

Walk up the paved path to the right (east) of the restrooms until you see a dirt trail on your right heading north. Get on the trail and walk until you come to the junction with the Sourdough Ridge Nature Trail. Turn left (northwest) onto the nature trail and walk 0.2 mile to the Sourdough Ridge Trail. Turn left (west) onto the Sourdough Ridge Trail.

While you are walking along this trail, you can see the Cascades to your right; on really clear days you can even see Mount Baker. Mount Rainier also looks magnificent from Sourdough Ridge. You will walk a total of 0.3 mile along the ridge, 0.6 mile from the Sunrise Complex, to the Huckleberry Creek Trail on your right, heading northwest. Stay to the left and on the Sourdough Ridge Trail for another 0.8 mile to the junction with Burroughs Mountain Trail. Directly before the junction, you pass Frozen Lake to your right (north). As the signs tell you, Frozen Lake is a domestic water supply; the National Park Service has fenced in the lake to avoid possible human contamination. The fence is not very aesthetically pleasing, but it is necessary.

Once you have reached the five-trail junction, take the Burroughs Mountain Trail, which heads southwest. Steep snowfields cover this trail into August in some years. Sturdy boots and an ice ax are recommended. The trail up to the first hump of Burroughs Mountain gains about 200 feet and travels through alpine terrain. The vegetation in this area is very fragile and susceptible to human impact. Please stay on the trail to avoid damaging the delicate ecosystem.

From Burroughs Mountain, you can see Old Desolate to the northwest and Berkeley Park to the north. Old Desolate is a barren plateau that sticks out among forested hills. It is quite a contrast to the bright wildflowers that fill Berkeley Park.

When you reach the first hump of Burroughs Mountain, 0.7 mile from Frozen Lake, turn left (east). To the south is the Emmons Glacier, the largest glacier in the contiguous United States. A better view of the glacier comes from the glacier overlook, 1.0 mile away. It is all downhill to the overlook and to Sunrise Camp.

You can see the entire Emmons Glacier and the beginning of the White River from the glacial overlook. Goat Island Mountain towers above both these natural wonders. The White River originates from the Emmons Glacier and is filled with sediment and glacial flour. Notice that there are several pools in the valley below. These pools appear seafoam green due to the large concentration of sediment suspended in their waters. The sun reflects light off the cloudy waters to produce this gorgeous color. It is amazing to imagine that the Emmons Glacier once filled the valley below.

Global warming has reduced the glacier to its present size, but all glaciers in the park are currently advancing.

From the glacial overlook, continue heading downhill to Sunrise Camp until you intersect the Sunrise Rim Trail. To your left, an administrative road heads north and passes Sunrise Camp. Continue going east, but on the Sunrise Rim Trail instead of the Burroughs Mountain Trail.

After hiking 0.2 mile east on the Sunrise Rim Trail, a total of 3.6 miles into your hike, Shadow Lake appears to the left. Previous hikers have greatly damaged the area around Shadow Lake, the water source for Sunrise Camp. Again, please stay on the trail to reduce your personal impact on the lake.

The remainder of the loop travels through the subalpine meadows of Yakima Park. In July and early August, Yakima Park is filled with a variety of wildflowers. At times you can see Goat Island Mountain and the Emmons Glacier from the trail. The trail is flat until you intersect the Wonderland Trail, and then it travels gradually uphill all the way to the Sunrise Complex parking lot.

Miles and Directions

0.0 Start from the Sunrise parking lot, follow the paved path to the right (east) of the restrooms, heading north. Don't let the road heading off to the left (west) tempt you; stay on the main trail, heading north past the informative display.

0.1 The Sourdough Ridge Nature Trail forks; stay to the left (northwest) toward Frozen Lake and Mount Fremont.

0.3 Reach the top of Sourdough Ridge and the junction with the Sourdough Ridge Nature Trail. Take a left (west) onto the trail.

0.6 Bypass the steep Huckleberry Creek Trail on your right (north).

1.4 Just beyond Frozen Lake, come to the junction of five trails. Take the Burroughs Mountain Trail, heading southwest.

2.4 In just 1.0 mile, go over the First Burroughs Mountain and reach the junction with the southern section of the Sunrise Loop. At the junction take a left (east) toward Sunrise Camp.

3.4 At the junction with the Sunrise Rim Trail, continue east, ignoring the administrative road on your left.

3.6 Just beyond Sunrise Camp, come to Shadow Lake.

4.4 Beyond Shadow Lake, reach another trail junction. This time, the Wonderland Trail is splitting off to your right (south). Continue east toward Sunrise.

4.9 Arrive back at the Sunrise parking lot.

25 Green Lake and Ranger Falls

An easy hike through old-growth forest travels past the gushing waters of Ranger Falls to a small, quaint emerald-green lake in the northwestern region of the park.

Start: Green Lake trailhead.
Distance: 3.6-mile out-and-back.
Approximate hiking time: 2 to 2.5 hours.
Elevation gain: 1,000 feet.
Seasons: May through October.
Nearest town: Wilkeson.
Fees and permits: $10.00 vehicle or $5.00 individual entry fee (seven days); $30.00 annual entry fee.

Maps: USGS: Mowich Lake; Trails Illustrated Mount Rainier National Park; Astronaut's Vista: Mount Rainier National Park, Washington; Earthwalk Press Hiking Map & Guide.
Trail contacts: Wilkeson Wilderness Information Center, (360) 829-5127.
Trail conditions: www.nps.gov/mora/trail/tr_cnd.htm; weather, www.nps.gov/mora/current/weather.htm.

Finding the trailhead: From the Carbon River Entrance Station (see Getting There), drive 3.0 miles east on Carbon River Road. The Green Lake trailhead is well marked by Ranger Creek to the right (south) and a small parking lot to the left (north). The Green Lake trailhead has few available spaces. Cars often line the road, parked on either side. *DeLorme: Washington Atlas and Gazetteer:* Page 48 A2.

Special considerations: The Carbon River Road may be open only to high-clearance vehicles after washouts have eaten up portions of the road. This road often washes out and has been known to close altogether. Call ahead, or check the Mount Rainier Web site for current conditions.

The Hike

The hike to Green Lake attracts many late-spring hikers because the snow clears earlier on this trail than most others in the park. Its traffic may lessen as the other trails open, but the trail's charm does not.

Dense, green rain forest and the gurgling sound of streams surround you as you ascend this moderate hill. After only 1.0 mile, the gurgling becomes churning. A very short jaunt to the left (east) leads you to a close-up view of Ranger Falls; the right takes you to Green Lake.

Only 0.5 mile beyond Ranger Falls on the way to Green Lake, you must cross Ranger Creek. No fording is necessary, but the footlog with only wire for a grip gets a bit slippery when wet, so cross carefully.

Less than 0.3 mile beyond the bridge, you come upon Green Lake. One glance, and the inspiration for the name becomes apparent. Surrounded by evergreens, the water reflects their emerald hue. The surrounding mountains shelter the water, keeping it placid. From a small clearing at the

Green Lake and Ranger Falls

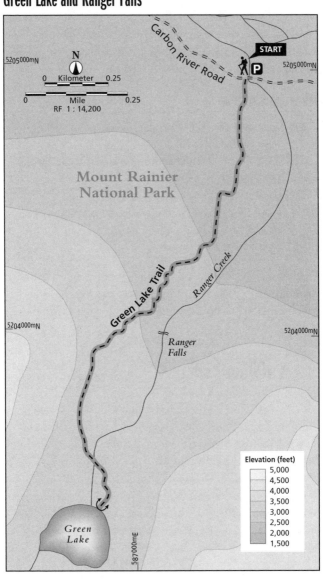

Green Lake Trail

Carbon River Road

START

P

Mount Rainier
National Park

Ranger Creek

Ranger
Falls

Green
Lake

5205000mN

5205000mN

5204000mN

5204000mN

587000mE

N

Kilometer
0   0.25

Mile
0   0.25
RF 1 : 14,200

Elevation (feet)
5,000
4,500
4,000
3,500
3,000
2,500
2,000
1,500

trail's end, a nice view of Tolmie Peak can be seen across the lake. No trails run around the lake for further exploration, but the small clearing is a good place to picnic or just rest before descending along the same path.

Miles and Directions

0.0 Start at the Green Lake trailhead. Follow the trail uphill until you reach Ranger Falls.

1.0 A small spur trail to Ranger Falls heads left (east). Continue right (south) on the Green Lake Trail.

1.5 Cross the footlog over Ranger Creek.

1.8 Reach Green Lake. Rest a bit or enjoy a picnic before retracing your steps.

3.6 Arrive back at the trailhead.

Option: If you would rather not hike the full 3.6 miles, turning back at Ranger Falls shortens the hike to only 2.0 miles round–trip. The falls still make the effort worthwhile.

26 Tolmie Peak

This very popular hike travels through forest and meadow to a fire lookout atop Tolmie Peak, which offers a spectacular view of the northwestern side of Mount Rainier. The trail also takes you by serene Eunice Lake, a lake surrounded by jutting peaks and subalpine forest.

Start: Mowich Lake.
Distance: 6.4-mile out-and-back.
Approximate hiking time: 2.5 to 4.5 hours.

Elevation gain: 1,020 feet.
Seasons: Mid-July through September.
Nearest town: Wilkeson.

Fees and permits: $10.00 vehicle or $5.00 individual entry fee (seven days); $30.00 annual entry fee.

Maps: USGS: Golden Lakes and Mowich Lake; Trails Illustrated Mount Rainier National Park; Astronaut's Vista: Mount Rainier National Park, Washington; Earthwalk Press Hiking Map & Guide.

Trail contacts: Wilkeson Wilderness Information Center, (360) 829-5127.
Mowich Ranger Station, (360) 829-2127.

Trail conditions: www.nps.gov/mora/trail/tr_cnd.htm; weather, www.nps.gov/mora/current/weather.htm.

Finding the trailhead: From Wilkeson drive 9.0 miles south on Washington Highway 165. Where Carbon River Road joins in, stay to the right on Highway 165. The pavement ends 3.2 miles beyond the intersection. Drive along a dirt road for 8.8 miles to reach the park boundary; pause here to pay the entry fee at the fee station. Continue another 5.3 miles to Mowich Lake Campground, which has a small parking lot. Many trails originate here; the trail to Tolmie Peak (Wonderland Trail) will be to your immediate left. *DeLorme: Washington Atlas and Gazetteer:* Page 48 A1.

The Hike

The hike to Tolmie Peak is one of the most popular in the park for many reasons. Neither too long nor too rigorous, it provides the opportunity to explore subalpine forests and a serene lake, as well as the opportunity to catch a breathtaking panorama of Mount Rainier.

Tolmie Peak and Tolmie Peak Trail are named for Dr. William Fraser Tolmie. This doctor, led by Nisqually headman Lahalet, was the first recorded non-Native American to approach Mount Rainier. Unlike others to follow him, he desired not to summit Mount Rainier but rather to collect

Tolmie Peak

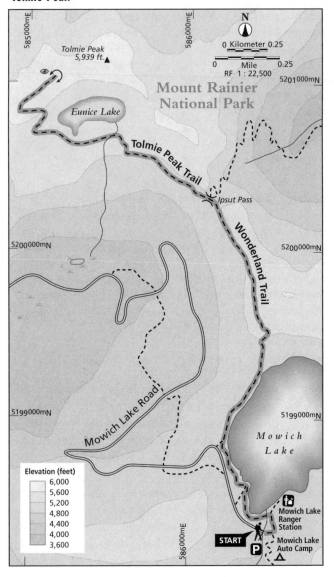

herbs for medicinal purposes and simply to enjoy the capti-vating scenery. Records indicate that he ascended all the way to Hessong Rock.

From the Mowich Lake parking lot, go to the Wonder-land Trail, which runs along the west side of Mowich Lake. There are several paths down to this trail, but the only trail that runs north-south along Mowich Lake is the Wonder-land Trail. Head north on the Wonderland Trail. The trail hugs the west side of Mowich Lake for about 0.5 mile before leaving the lake and heading north. After reaching the top of a small hill, continue on flat terrain to the junction with the Tolmie Peak Trail. At the junction turn left (north-west).

After turning, you immediately begin to descend steeply. At the bottom of this hill, the trail forks. The trail to the left is an unmaintained social trail created by those eager to see a small waterfall only a few paces off the beaten path. Stay to the right (north) to continue the journey to Eunice Lake and Tolmie Peak.

At this point the trail begins a steep climb via switch-backs. As you approach Eunice Lake, you may step into a field blanketed by avalanche lilies, as we did in mid-July. Jutting peaks and subalpine forest surround the lake's aqua blue waters.

A sign points the way to Tolmie Peak. Stay to the left (west) on the marked trail around the lake. Those who have ventured off have spoiled the land, killing the fragile meadow plants and creating an array of ugly paths to the lake.

The trail reaches the northwestern part of the lake and then begins to ascend by means of long switchbacks up to the Tolmie Peak Lookout. The view from the lookout is spectacular. To the north you see an expanse of rolling mountains. To the south is one of the best panoramic views of Mount Rainier available in the park.

The more adventurous can carefully walk the unmaintained trail along a ridge for 0.1 mile to the true Tolmie Peak. The trail is not steep, but it is rocky and a bit tricky at points.

Miles and Directions

0.0 Start at the Mowich Lake parking lot. Find the Wonderland Trail, which runs along the west side of Mowich Lake. There are several paths down to this trail, but the only trail that runs north-south along Mowich Lake is the Wonderland Trail. Head north on the Wonderland Trail.

1.5 At the Tolmie Peak Trail junction, turn left (northwest).

2.4 Stay to the left (west) on the marked trail around Eunice Lake.

3.1 Reach the Tolmie Peak Lookout and the end of the maintained trail.

3.2 A steep and rocky unmaintained trail takes you to the top of Tolmie Peak. Carefully make your way back to the main trail, and then head back to the trailhead.

6.4 Arrive back at the parking lot.

Option: Rather than hiking all the way to the top of Tolmie Peak, go only as far as Eunice Lake. This option cuts 1.6 miles off the total distance. Eunice Lake is absolutely delightful, as are the fields of avalanche lilies that bloom in July.

27 Spray Falls

This short, relatively flat hike travels through beautiful forest to striking Spray Falls. From the top of these tall falls, water sprays out, leaving the air misty and raining down on the colorful wildflowers lining Spray Creek below the falls.

Start: Mowich Lake.
Distance: 4.0-mile out-and-back.
Approximate hiking time: 1.5 to 2.5 hours.
Elevation gain: Minimal.
Seasons: Early July through September.
Nearest town: Wilkeson.
Fees and permits: $10.00 vehicle or $5.00 individual entry fee (seven days); $30.00 annual entry fee. Wilderness Camping Permits free—reservations recommended ($20 fee).

Maps: USGS: Mowich Lake; Trails Illustrated Mount Rainier National Park; Astronaut's Vista: Mount Rainier National Park, Washington; Earthwalk Press Hiking Map & Guide.
Trail contacts: Wilkeson Wilderness Information Center, (360) 829-5127.
Trail conditions: www.nps.gov/mora/trail/tr_cnd.htm; weather, www.nps.gov/mora/current/weather.htm.

Finding the trailhead: From Wilkeson drive 9.0 miles south on Highway 165 until the road forks. Stay to the right (south) at this fork, the way to Mowich Lake. After 3.2 miles the road turns into a well-maintained dirt road, although it can be very slippery when muddy. Follow this road for another 8.8 miles to the Paul Peak trailhead on the right (south) side of the road. Pause here to pay the entrance fee at the fee station, then continue south and east 5.3 miles to Mowich Lake, a total of 26.3 miles from Wilkeson. The parking lot is fairly big, but on sunny weekends you might have to park along the road. *DeLorme: Washington Atlas and Gazetteer:* Page 48 A1.

The Hike

This hike has no significant elevation gain, but it trundles over rolling hills all the way to Spray Falls. A trail construction crew named Spray Falls in 1883 because they felt that the cascading falls broke "into a mass of spray." The well-maintained, heavily used trail winds through beautiful forest. Expect to see many other park visitors; please reduce your impact by staying on the trail.

Head to the south end of Mowich Lake, past the restrooms and Mowich Lake Campground to the Wonderland Trail. Go south on the Wonderland Trail for a little over 0.2 mile to the junction with the Spray Park Trail. Go left (southeast) when the Spray Park Trail forks off from the Wonderland Trail. About a mile after the junction, a short spur trail from the junction leads to an overlook from Eagle Cliff, a total of 1.5 miles into your hike. You can see the North Mowich Glacier clearly from the lookout.

At 0.3 mile past the lookout, you will see the signs for Eagle's Roost Camp. Eagle's Roost Camp is less than 0.1 mile away and south of the Spray Park Trail. Just beyond the camp is the junction with the Spray Falls Trail. Go right (southeast) onto the Spray Falls Trail, which goes 0.1 mile to Spray Creek and Spray Falls.

The falls drop roughly 160 feet. At the top of the falls, the water sprays off the mossy rocks, leaving the air misty and cool. Lewis and yellow monkeyflowers line Spray Creek, adding to the beauty of this natural wonder.

Miles and Directions

0.0 Start at Mowich Lake. Head to the south end of the lake, past the restrooms and Mowich Lake Campground to the

Spray Falls

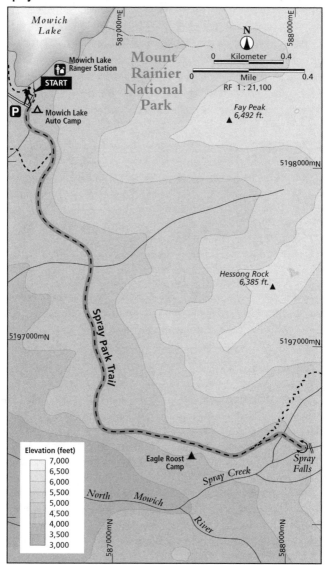

Mowich Lake

Mowich Lake Ranger Station

START

P

Mowich Lake Auto Camp

Mount Rainier National Park

N

Kilometer

0   0.4

Mile

0   0.4

RF 1 : 21,100

Fay Peak 6,492 ft.

587000mE

588000mE

5198000mN

Hessong Rock 6,385 ft.

Spray Park Trail

5197000mN

5197000mN

Eagle Roost Camp

Spray Creek

Spray Falls

North

Mowich

River

587000mN

588000mN

Elevation (feet)

7,000
6,500
6,000
5,500
5,000
4,500
4,000
3,500
3,000

Wonderland Trail. Go south on the Wonderland Trail for a little over 0.2 mile to the junction with the Spray Park Trail.

0.2 At the junction with the Spray Park Trail, go left (southeast) onto the trail.

1.8 On the right, the spur trail to Eagle's Roost Camp leaves the trail, heading south. Stay to the left (east).

1.9 Turn right, heading southeast at the junction with Spray Falls Trail.

2.0 The trail travels next to Spray Creek; Spray Falls lies at the end of the trail. Enjoy the falls before retracing your steps.

4.0 Arrive back at the Mowich Lake.

28 Chenuis Falls

Despite its shortness, this hike takes you through a variety of natural wonders. The hike begins by traversing the wide, pebbly riverbed of Carbon River and continues through an old-growth forest to beautiful, cascading Chenuis Falls.

Start: Chenuis Falls trailhead.
Distance: 0.4-mile out-and-back.
Approximate hiking time: 30 minutes.
Elevation gain: Minimal.
Seasons: May through October.
Nearest town: Wilkeson.
Fees and permits: $10.00 vehicle or $5.00 individual entry fee (seven days); $30.00 annual entry fee.
Maps: USGS: Mowich Lake;

Trails Illustrated Mount Rainier National Park; Astronaut's Vista: Mount Rainier National Park, Washington; Earthwalk Press Hiking Map & Guide.
Trail contacts: Wilkeson Wilderness Information Center, (360) 829-5127.
Trail conditions: www.nps.gov/mora/trail/tr_cnd.htm; weather, www.nps.gov/mora/current/weather.htm.

Finding the trailhead: From the Carbon River Entrance Station (see Getting There), drive 3.5 miles to the Chenuis Falls trailhead, located on the left (north). Limited parking is available. *DeLorme: Washington Atlas and Gazetteer:* Page 48 A2.

Special considerations: Check ahead to make sure the footlogs over Carbon River have not washed out before starting this hike. These footlogs often wash out and need to be replaced.

The Carbon River Road may be open only to high-clearance vehicles after washouts have eaten up portions of the road. This road often washes out and has been known to close altogether. Call ahead, or check the Mount Rainier Web site for current conditions.

The Hike

From the trailhead descend the steep side of the riverbank to the first crossing of the Carbon River. There may be up to seven footlogs crossing the many channels of the Carbon River, but the location and number change according to how the river reroutes itself. Continue traveling northeast toward the north bank of the river, making sure to look up the riverbed toward Mount Rainier for fantastic views of Crescent Mountain in front of Mount Rainier.

The trail, consisting of gray sand and river rock from the Carbon River, is sometimes difficult to follow, even though the Park Service tries to outline it in rock. If you continue heading toward the footlogs, it will lead you all the way to the north bank. At this point the trail heads into beautiful old-growth forest with ferns, devil's club, and lichen-covered trees lining the path. Continue hiking along the trail. You will pass an unmaintained trail to your left, but continue hiking north along the main trail to a small overlook with a view of Chenuis Falls. The unmaintained trail that you just

Chenuis Falls

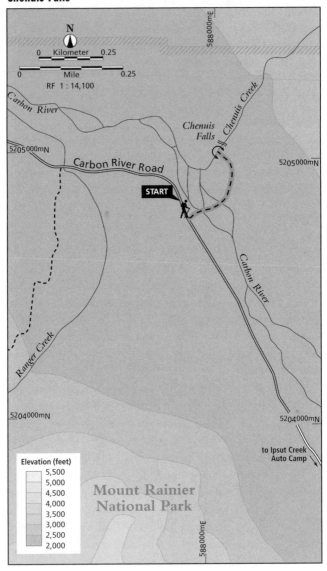

passed also takes you to the falls; many people take that trail on their return trip, making the hike a lollipop.

Take the time to enjoy the clear waters of Chenuis Falls as they cascade down the smooth rocks. The falls are at a gentle slope, allowing the waters to weave between large rocks. Just past your viewing point, the clear waters from Chenuis Creek join the silty waters of the Carbon River.

Miles and Directions

0.0 Start at Chenuis Falls Trailhead. Hike through the riverbed to the north side, using the footlogs as your guide.

0.1 Enter the forest. You will immediately pass an old, unmaintained trail to the right, heading east. Continue north. You will pass another unmaintained trail to your left, but continue to the right (north).

0.2 The trail takes you to a small overlook with a view of Chenuis Falls. Either retrace your steps or make a small lollipop by taking the unmaintained trail back to the main trail.

0.4 Arrive back at the trailhead.

29 Twin Firs Loop

This short loop takes you through an old-growth, low-elevation forest. Along the trail you will see a variety of flora such as vine maple, skunk cabbage, giant ferns, mossy logs, Douglas fir, western hemlock, and western red cedar, as well as numerous squirrels darting across the trail.

Start: Twin Firs Loop trailhead.
Distance: 0.4-mile loop.
Approximate hiking time: 20 minutes.
Elevation gain: Minimal.
Seasons: May through October.
Nearest town: Ashford.
Fees and permits: $10.00 vehicle or $5.00 individual entry fee (seven days); $30.00 annual entry fee.

Maps: USGS: Mount Wow; Trails Illustrated Mount Rainier National Park; Astronaut's Vista: Mount Rainier National Park, Washington; Earthwalk Press Hiking Map & Guide.
Trail contacts: Longmire Wilderness Information Center: (360) 569–HIKE (4453).
Trail conditions: www.nps.gov/mora/trail/tr_cnd.htm; weather, www.nps.gov/mora/current/weather.htm.

Finding the trailhead: From the Nisqually Entrance Station (see Getting There), drive east for 4.5 miles on the Longmire-Paradise Road. You will see a turnout on the left of the road. If you reach the Longmire Historic District, you have gone too far. *DeLorme: Washington Atlas and Gazetteer:* Page 48 C2.

The Hike

At the trailhead take the time to read a wonderful exhibit describing the flora of low-elevation forests. Through pictures and written description, the exhibit recommends ways

Twin Firs Loop

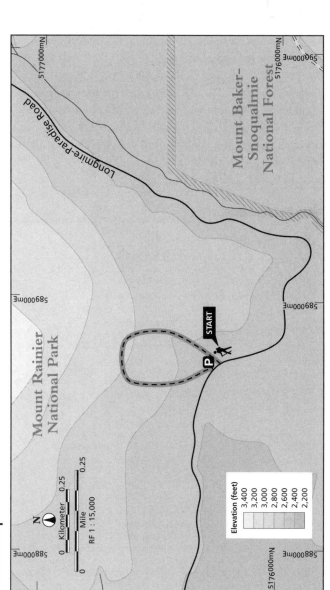

Mount Rainier National Park

Mount Baker-Snoqualmie National Forest

Longmire-Paradise Road

START

P

Elevation (feet)
3,400
3,200
3,000
2,800
2,600
2,400
2,200

N

Kilometer
0   0.25

Mile
0   0.25

RF 1 : 15,000

5177000mN
5176000mN
590000mE
589000mE
588000mE
5178000mN
5176000mN

to differentiate between the Douglas fir, western hemlock, and western red cedar.

The trail weaves around majestic trees, some fallen and some standing tall. You will see mossy logs and big ferns lining both sides of the trail. Less than halfway into your hike, a log takes you across a small creek to where the trail becomes steeper. You will cross this gurgling creek again just before you return to the Longmire-Paradise road, directly west of where you begin your hike.

Miles and Directions

0.0   Start at the Twin Firs Loop trailhead.

0.4   Return to the Longmire Paradise Road.

About the Authors

Mary Skjelset and Heidi Schneider are still the youngest author team to complete a FalconGuide. Heidi is currently studying medicine at Oregon Health Sciences University, with a strong commitment to community service. Her childhood was spent exploring the wilderness in and around Montana. Heidi continues to derive strength and spirituality from nature. Also from Montana, Mary appreciates the wild side of life. After graduating college and working with an environmental organization in the Czech Republic, she settled in Oregon and now attends law school at Lewis and Clark College.